CAREERS FOR

PERFECTIONISTS

& Other Meticulous Types

Careers for You Series

CAREERS FOR

PERFECTIONISTS

& Other Meticulous Types

BLYTHE CAMENSON

SECOND EDITION

New York Chicago San Francisco Lisbon London Madrid Mexico City
Milan New Delhi San Juan Seoul Singapore Sydney Toronto

The *McGraw·Hill* Companies

Library of Congress Cataloging-in-Publication Data

Camenson, Blythe.
　Careers for perfectionists & other meticulous types / by Blythe Camenson —
2nd ed.
　　　p.　cm.　— (McGraw-Hill careers for you series)
　　　ISBN 0-07-146778-5 (alk. paper)
　　　1. Vocational guidance.　2. Perfectionism (Personality trait).　I. Title.
　II. Title: Careers for perfectionists and other meticulous types.

　HF5381.C2532 2007
　331.702—dc22　　　　　　　　　　　　　　　　　　　2006014338

1　2　3　4　5　6　7　8　9　0　　DOC/DOC　0　9　8　7　6

ISBN-13: 978-0-07-146778-0
ISBN-10:　　0-07-146778-5

McGraw-Hill books are available at special quantity discounts to use as premiums and
sales promotions, or for use in corporate training programs. For more information,
please write to the Director of Special Sales, Professional Publishing, McGraw-Hill,
Two Penn Plaza, New York, NY 10121-2298. Or contact your local bookstore.

This book is printed on acid-free paper.

*To Jan Goldberg, a friend
and colleague, and to
Marshall J. Cook,
a perfect gentleman*

Contents

Acknowledgments

The author would like to thank the following perfectionists for providing information about their careers:

Peter Benton
Kent Brinkley
Susan Broadwater-Chen
Diane Camerlo
Lisa Eagleson-Roever
Joan Gardner
Sara Goodman
Rod Stafford Hagwood
David Martin
Nancy McVicar
Valarie Neiman
George T. Ragsdale
Moana Re
Joel Witt

The editors would like to thank Denise Frank for preparing this revised edition.

CHAPTER ONE

Scrutinizing the Options

D o you cross every *t* and dot every *i*? Is your house as neat as a pin, your closets and drawers organized, a place for everything and everything in its place? Do you have a penchant for taking things apart, examining the tiny bits and pieces, and reassembling them into proper working order? Do you feel that there is a right and a wrong way to do things and no room for error or deviation? If any of this sounds familiar, then this is the right book for you!

Although some people might call you fussy, your special qualities are highly valued in a number of settings, particularly in the world of work. There are certain jobs that require a meticulous mind, something that not just everyone is lucky enough to possess. Wouldn't you love a chance to get your ducks in a row—and get paid for it? *Careers for Perfectionists* will lead you toward careers that will allow you to put your talents to good use. From lawyers and tax accountants to editors and art restorers, this book features a range of careers, including one that's sure to be perfect for you.

What Makes a Perfectionist?

So many of the nouns and adjectives that describe a perfectionist carry negative connotations. After all, who would enjoy being called a *nitpicker* or a *critical fusspot*? But true perfectionists don't allow themselves to be rattled by silly labels. They know that their eye for detail and their need to solve exasperating problems have contributed to their success in the workplace.

Perhaps a fussbudget catches a bit more flak than the easygoing devil-may-care types, but whatever behaviors constitute a perfectionist's repertoire, on the job they are seen with a whole different set of nouns and adjectives: *excellence, incomparability, flawlessness*, and *ideal*. Perfectionists are purists; they are uncompromising workers who like to undertake tasks thoroughly and properly. Because of their attention to detail, perfectionists are nearly always excellent at whatever they put their minds to—not a bad lot to be grouped together with.

Career Possibilities

Perfectionists possess qualities above and beyond an attention to detail. They are as diverse as the areas of interest they might explore. Some are thrilled by research or enjoy working with and manipulating numbers or words. Others find their niche working with the law, where contracts and other legal documents demand a perfectionist's touch. Still others might find satisfaction working with their hands as art restorers, surveyors, mapmakers, or architects. The skills of the perfectionist also translate well to the technical world, where careers in the many branches of engineering are waiting.

Perfectionists are excellent fact finders; some apply their talents to sifting through an incredible amount of information in order to locate a specific bit of knowledge. And who would make a better efficiency expert than a true perfectionist?

Although most employers expect a high performance level from employees, there are some careers where high performance just isn't enough. Perfection is very much necessary—and demanded. But that doesn't cause a problem for you, the career-oriented perfectionist. You strive for no less than perfection in everything you do.

While there are scores of jobs that would be well suited to the perfectionist, space limitations allow us to cover only a few of them. We've tried to include a range of careers in this book. Each chapter features a very different type of job to give you an idea of the diversity of choices available to you. Your options are many, so be sure to take your time and explore career possibilities before deciding on one. This book is an excellent first step in your career exploration. In it, you will learn about the following careers that are ideal for perfectionists.

Number Crunchers

You received the Best Math Student award in high school. You may go on to college and get a bachelor's degree in math or perhaps even an M.B.A. Statistics makes complete sense to you, and your school counselors are steering you toward a career as an actuary or an accountant. And that might just be the perfect choice for you. Although accountants sometimes get a bad rap and are the butt of some jokes, in real life, they are often very influential people who are integral assets to businesses, the government, and individuals. Chapter 2 describes what it's like to work as a perfectionist in the world of figures.

Lawyers

In the world of television, Perry Mason is probably the best-known lawyer in this country. His clients are always innocent, he always gets them off, and he always nabs the real criminal in the process. But real life does not always follow the imagination of television writers. If you decide to pursue a career in criminal law, many of your clients will not be innocent, and you might not be able to get them all off. Some you'd even rather not represent. However, in our justice system, everyone is innocent until proven guilty, and everyone is entitled to legal defense.

Lawyers shape the rules and regulations that govern how our society functions, which is no small task. After years of study, they put their practice to work in a variety of settings. Criminal lawyers operate their own practices, work for private law firms, or represent clients under the auspices of the public defender's office. Lawyers who work for state attorneys general, prosecutors, and courts play a key role in the criminal justice system. At the federal level, attorneys investigate cases for the Department of Justice or other agencies. Also, lawyers at every government level help develop programs, draft laws, interpret legislation, establish enforcement procedures, and argue civil and criminal cases on behalf of the government.

But criminal trial work is not the only option open to lawyers. Just as doctors gear their careers toward a particular specialty, so do lawyers. Chapter 3 will introduce you to a variety of law specializations—and they all require the talents of a perfectionist. Most of the work is detail oriented, some of it is frustrating, and some involves great pressure—but there's no greater reward than seeing justice at work.

Architects

Architecture can be beautiful, functional, or both. As Frank Lloyd Wright once said, "form follows function" means that the design and look of a building should be one with the function or use of the building and its surrounding areas. This is achieved to greater or lesser extent depending on the skills of the architects. In fact, architects have the ability to shape the look of whole cities. Perhaps the best example of this is Chicago, which was essentially razed in the Great Fire of 1871. Architects, learning from past mistakes, were able to redesign the city, which features some of the best modern architecture in the world.

Architects work with individuals and companies to design buildings and other structures. Some restore historic buildings, create mixed-use building in which people both live and work, and construct art museums and amphitheaters. Architects provide a wide variety of professional services to individuals and organizations planning a construction project. They may be involved in all phases of development, from the initial discussion of general ideas with the client through construction. Their duties require a number of detail-oriented skills, such as design, engineering, management, communication, and more, all of which will be discussed in Chapter 4.

Surveyors and Mapmakers

Have you ever noticed individuals on sidewalks or the sides of roads peering into a tripod-like instrument? These are land surveyors, who take measurements of areas in order to help with urban and rural planning and maintenance. Land surveyors work with mapmakers to construct an exact and detailed description of a space or place. Surveyors and mapmakers work in both remote and heavily populated areas. Architectural, engineering, and surveying firms employ them, although many also work for federal, state, and local government agencies, including the Bureau of Land Management, the Army Corps of Engineers, the Forest Service, highway departments, and urban planning agencies.

Chapter 5 will tell you more about these workers who map the earth.

Engineers

Ever wonder who came up with the latest design of those sleek and space-age sports shoes you've been coveting? Or what about your favorite ride at the closest amusement park—you know, the one that takes you up several stories and then drops you off the edge? Both of these products come from the minds of engineers.

Engineers work to find economical solutions to practical technical problems. They design machinery, products, systems, and processes for the highest-level performance attainable. In addition to their design work, they also develop products, test or maintain them, and even estimate the time and cost required to complete them. Chapter 6 features the work of engineers, those methodical types who have their hands on everything from the latest car designs to subway systems.

Art Conservators and Restorers

Nothing demands more painstaking accuracy than restoring a valuable work of art. Restoration is often conceived of as trying to bring something back to its original condition. Sometimes, however, restoration work is intended to slow down further deterioration. Art conservators and restorers are part sleuths, determining how a work of art has been damaged, and part artists, using a variety of techniques to reveal an object's hidden beauty. This is an excellent career path for those who appreciate art but do not have the inclination or talent to create it themselves. Working with such objects allows art conservators and restorers to make valuable contributions to our culture. Chapter 7 describes these fascinating jobs in detail.

Researchers

Tracing a family tree, surfing the Web for an obscure fact, and helping a doctoral candidate find information to complete a dissertation are all research-based activities, and detail-oriented people willingly sink their teeth into such meaty projects. The career options for the person who gets a charge out of sifting through mountains of books, microfilm, or online databases are many and varied. In research, there is a range of settings in which to work—from the hallowed halls of a university or library to a home office—and a range of types of research to conduct, including genealogical research and higher-level scientific research. Regardless of what kind of research you're interested in conducting, Chapter 8 has the information you need to determine whether this is truly the area for you.

Writers and Editors

Writers, editors, and proofreaders all understand the meaning of the word *perfection*. Just as accountants are meticulous in the way they handle numbers, so are writers and related professionals when it comes to dealing with words. That's because writing, revising, polishing, and searching for errors are all activities that require a strict attention to detail. A large number of employment options are available to these word managers, including working for publishing companies and literary agencies, working for magazines and newspapers, and establishing your own home-based freelance office. Chapter 9 will give you more information about the high-prestige world of the publishing industry.

Choosing Your Field

People who perform exacting work give of themselves in many capacities, providing a variety of valuable services. If you're reading this book, chances are you're already considering one of the many careers well suited to perfectionists. But perhaps you'd like to know more about the working conditions the different fields offer or which area would best suit your personality, skills, and lifestyle. If so, there are several factors to consider when deciding which sector to pursue. Each field carries with it different levels of responsibility and commitment. To identify occupations that will match your expectations, you need to know what each job entails.

Conducting the following exercise will help you pinpoint the fields that interest you and eliminate those that would clearly be the wrong choice. First, ask yourself the following questions and make note of your answers. Then, compare your requirements to the information provided in each chapter.

- How much time are you willing to commit to training and education? Some skills can be learned on the job; others take only a year or two of some form of training; still others require a bachelor's or master's degree. Consider whether you like reading and book learning, working with equations or computers, or learning in a more show-and-tell or hands-on style. As you read each chapter, note what type of training is required for each job and whether that corresponds with the way you learn best.

- What kind of setting do you want to work in? Do you want to work behind a desk, either at home or in a busy office, or would you prefer to be out and about, surveying property or supervising the construction of a building? Whether it be in the laboratory, library, or the great outdoors, you'll have to like the kind of setting in which you spend the majority of your week. If, for example, you can't stand the thought of being cooped up in an office all day, then you'll want to think twice about working in the kind of job in which the office is the chief working space.

- Can you handle a certain amount of stress, or would you prefer a more low-key job? Some people thrive on stress and feel charged up when fielding the demands of many. Others, however, prefer jobs that don't require such an intense emotional commitment. What type are you?

- How much money do you expect to earn starting out and after you have a few years' experience under your belt? Salaries and earnings vary greatly in each chosen profession, and, while money is not the only benefit offered by the various jobs, it can be a substantial perk to the profession. Consider how important money is to you. Perhaps you value nonmonetary rewards, such as satisfaction and contributing to society, more than a paycheck. If so, then you may find lower-paying professions more suitable to your taste.

- Are you a leader or a team-player? Do you want to be your own boss, or will you be content as a salaried employee? Keep in mind that with the independence of management and leadership comes the responsibility and stress of being the one in charge. Also, how much independence do you require? Do you prefer to work on your own or with a group on projects? Some jobs are fairly isolated, while others involve navigating the terrain of working with various personality types. Know your strengths and weaknesses, likes and dislikes in this area.

Knowing your expectations and then comparing them to the realities of the work will help you make informed choices, so be thorough in your responses to these questions.

For More Information

Unfortunately, we cannot cover even a fraction of the detail that would be required for you to learn all you need to know about the careers in this book. Consequently, we've provided extensive sources for additional information in the appendix material. In Appendix A, you will find professional associations for many of the career paths explored in this book. These associations and organizations offer a range of useful information. In Appendix B you will find resources for job hunting, including career-specific and general job-hunting sites. While you're probably not ready to launch your career just yet, these sites can offer you wonderful information for setting up a resume and reference list—never too early for that!—and for reading what employers are looking for in terms of experience and training for the kinds of jobs you're attracted to.

Whichever path you choose, you've taken a great first step: picking up this book and learning about careers for perfectionists.

CHAPTER TWO

Number Crunchers

There is probably no other field that demands perfection more than working with numbers. Where numbers, figures, and calculations are involved, there truly is a right way and a wrong way of doing things. Perhaps this is why mathematical subjects and tasks intimidate so many people. If you excel in math and find playing with calculations challenging, yet fun, then you're likely a person who would enjoy any number of careers working with numbers. If you're the kind of person who particularly enjoys the methodical nature of figuring out algebra and calculus equations, then you're definitely a perfectionist. If you have a head for figures, you will find that there are all kinds of career opportunities available for dedicated number crunchers.

In this chapter, we cover three main areas of the number-crunching professions—accountants and auditors, actuaries, and statisticians—although the skills these professionals use translate easily to a number of additional fields. Accountants and auditors design internal control systems and analyze financial data. Appraisers, budget officers, loan officers, financial analysts and managers, bank officers, actuaries, underwriters, tax collectors and revenue agents, FBI special agents, securities sales workers, and purchasing agents also find training in accounting invaluable to their work. Actuaries determine the probability of income or loss from various risk factors. Accountants, economists, financial analysts, mathematicians, rate analysts, risk managers, statisticians, and value engineers are other workers whose jobs involve related skills. There are numerous occupations that involve working with statistics, including actuaries, mathematicians, operations research analysts, computer programmers, computer systems analysts, engineers, economists, financial analysts, information scientists, life scientists, mathematicians, physical scientists, and social scientists. We'll begin by examining the work of accountants and auditors.

Accountants and Auditors

There are four major fields of accounting: public accounting, management accounting, government accounting, and internal auditing. Accountants and auditors in all fields do similar work. They prepare, analyze, and verify financial reports and taxes and monitor information systems that furnish this information to managers in all business, industrial, and government organizations, as well as to individuals. The differences are in for whom they work and the focus of the accounting. Within each field accountants often concentrate on one phase of accounting.

Public accountants generally run their own businesses or work for public accounting firms. They perform a broad range of accounting, auditing, tax, and consulting activities for their clients, who may be corporations, governments, nonprofit organizations, or individuals. Many public accountants concentrate on tax matters, such as preparing an individual's income tax returns and advising companies of the tax advantages and disadvantages of certain business decisions. Others concentrate on consulting and offer advice on matters such as employee health care benefits and compensation, the design of companies' accounting and data processing systems, and controls to safeguard assets. Some specialize in forensic accounting, which involves investigating and interpreting bankruptcies and other complex financial transactions. Still others work primarily in auditing, examining a client's financial statements and reporting to investors and authorities that they have been prepared and reported correctly.

Beginning public accountants usually start out by assisting a more senior accountant with his or her work for several clients. It usually takes a year or two to begin to advance to more independent positions, taking on clients of your own. After about five years, you should reach a senior level and have a new accountant assisting you with your work. If you're really good at your job, you may eventually become a supervisor, manager, or partner; open your own public accounting firm; or transfer to an executive position in management accounting or internal auditing in another firm.

Management accountants (also called industrial, corporate, or private accountants) record and analyze the financial information of the companies for which they work. Management accountants interpret the financial information corporate executives need to make sound business decisions. They also prepare financial reports for nonmanagement groups, including stockholders, creditors, regulatory agencies, and tax authorities. Within accounting departments, they may work in financial analysis, planning and budgeting, cost accounting, and other areas.

Management accountants often start as cost accountants, junior internal auditors, or trainees for other accounting positions. As they rise through the organization, they may advance to accounting manager, chief cost accountant, budget director, or manager of internal auditing. Some become controllers, treasurers, financial vice presidents, chief financial officers, or corporation presidents.

Government accountants and auditors work for federal, state, and local governments to maintain and examine the records of government agencies and audit private businesses and individuals whose activities are subject to government regulations or taxation. Government accountants see that revenues are received and expenditures are made in accordance with laws and regulations. Those working for the government may work in departments of financial management, financial institution examination, and budget analysis and administration. The Internal Revenue Service (IRS) is a major employer of accountants and auditors.

Internal auditors verify the accuracy of their organizations' records and check for mismanagement, waste, or fraud. This is an area that's rapidly growing in importance. As computer systems make information more timely and available, top management can base its decisions on actual data rather than personal observation. Internal auditors examine and evaluate their firms' financial and information systems, management procedures, and internal controls to ensure that records are accurate and controls are adequate to protect against fraud and waste. They also review company operations, evaluating their efficiency, effectiveness, and compliance with corporate policies and procedures, laws, and government regulations. There are many types of highly specialized internal auditors, such as electronic data processing auditors, environmental auditors, engineering auditors, legal auditors, insurance auditors, bank auditors, and health care auditors. In addition, a small number of trained accountants teach and conduct research at business and professional schools.

In general, public accountants, management accountants, and internal auditors have much occupational mobility. Practitioners often shift from public accounting into management accounting or internal auditing, or they might move between internal auditing and management accounting. It is less common for accountants and auditors to move from either management accounting or internal auditing into public accounting.

Computers

Computers are widely used in accounting and auditing. With the aid of special computer software packages, accountants summarize transactions in standard formats for financial records or organize data in special formats for financial analysis. These accounting packages are easily learned and require few specialized computer skills, greatly reducing the amount of tedious manual work associated with figures and records. Personal and laptop computers enable accountants and auditors in all fields, even those who work independently, to use their clients' computer systems and to extract information from large mainframe computers. A growing number of accountants and auditors have extensive computer skills and specialize in correcting problems with software or in developing software to meet unique data needs. For example, internal auditors may recommend controls for their organizations' computer systems to ensure the reliability of the systems and the integrity of the data. Along with your skill in working out numbers with a pencil on paper, you should become adept at using all manner of computer systems and new technologies.

Work Settings and Hours

Accountants and auditors hold an astounding 1.2 million jobs. They work in all types of firms and industries, but nearly one-third work for accounting, auditing, and bookkeeping firms or are self-employed. Most accountants and auditors are found in urban areas where public accounting firms and central or regional offices of businesses are concentrated.

Accountants and auditors generally work in offices, whether their own or the offices of their clients. Public accountants frequently visit clients while conducting audits and may spend much of their time on the road, carrying necessary paperwork in their briefcases. Self-employed accountants may be able to do part of their work at home. Accountants and auditors employed by large firms and government agencies may travel to perform audits at clients' places of business, branches of their firms, or government facilities.

The majority of accountants and auditors generally work a standard forty-hour week, but many work longer, particularly if they are self-employed and free to take on the work of as many clients as they choose. For example, about two out of five self-employed accountants and auditors work more than fifty hours per week, compared to one out of four wage and salary accountants and auditors. Tax specialists often work long hours during the tax season, which is in the spring, and may have a substantial amount of time off during the rest of the year. Employees of larger corporations have more reliable and steady work year-round. Some people choose to work part-time; in particular, accountants and auditors who teach at junior colleges, colleges, and universities may choose to work only part-time as accountants.

Job Outlook

The field of accounting and financial auditing is a growing one. In fact, according to the U.S. Department of Labor, Bureau of Labor Statistics (www.bls.gov), a division of the government that collects employment and job-related statistics, employment of accountants and auditors is expected to grow faster than average for all occupations through the year 2014. As the economy grows, the number of business establishments will increase, requiring more accountants and auditors to set up books, prepare taxes, and provide management advice. As these businesses grow, the amount of information developed by accountants and auditors regarding costs, expenditures, and taxes will increase as well. The growth of international business also has led to more demand for accounting services related to international trade and accounting rules, as well as to international mergers and acquisitions.

As a result of accounting scandals at several large corporate companies in recent years, Congress passed legislation in an effort to curb corporate accounting fraud. This legislation requires public companies to make sure that their financial accounting records and standards are accurate and reliable. It also holds the company's chief executive personally responsible for falsely reporting financial information. These legislative changes should lead to increased scrutiny of company finances and accounting procedures and should create opportunities for accountants and auditors, particularly CPAs, to audit financial records more thoroughly. In order to ensure that finances comply with the law before public accountants conduct audits, management accountants and internal auditors will increasingly be needed to discover and eliminate fraud. Also, in an effort to make government agencies more efficient and accountable, demand for government accountants should increase.

The recent focus on financial crimes, such as embezzlement, bribery, and securities fraud, will increase the demand for forensic accountants. Forensic accountants specialize in detecting illegal financial activity conducted by individuals, companies, and organized crime rings. Computer technology has made these crimes easier to commit, and they are on the rise. At the same time, the development of new computer software and electronic surveillance technology has made tracking down financial criminals easier. As success rates of investigations grow, demand also will grow for these financial crime fighters.

Training and Education

Most accountant and auditor positions require at least a bachelor's degree in accounting or a related field. Some employers even prefer applicants with a master's degree in accounting, or with a master's degree in business administration with a concentration in accounting. In addition, if you're good with computers and learn the software applications in accounting, you'll be a great asset to a future employer.

Previous experience in accounting or auditing will help you get a job. Many colleges offer students an opportunity to gain experience through summer or part-time internship programs conducted by public accounting or business firms. Working a few hours a week while you're in school will not only give you valuable experience, but you'll probably earn some spending money.

In order to get ahead, many people seek out professional recognition through certification or licensure. Certified public accountants (CPAs) are licensed by the state Board of Accountancy. This license to practice must be renewed regularly, which requires you to meet certain professional development qualifications; essentially, you'll need to take additional courses or participate in accounting-specific seminars.

Many accountants and auditors obtain other forms of credentials from professional societies on a voluntary basis. Voluntary certification tells employers that you have skills in a specialized field. In fact, you can obtain numerous types of certifications. Graduates from accredited colleges and universities who have worked for two years as internal auditors and have passed a four-part examination may earn the Certified Internal Auditor (CIA) designation from the Institute of Internal Auditors (www.theiia .org). The Information Systems Audit and Control Association (www.isaca.org) confers the Certified Information Systems Auditor (CISA) designation upon candidates who pass an examination and have five years of experience auditing information systems. These certifications are only two of the many you could obtain when you become a licensed CPA.

In order to succeed in this field, you must be good at mathematics and be able to analyze, compare, and interpret facts and figures quickly. You should also be able to clearly communicate the results of your work to clients and managers both verbally and in writing. It is essential that you are good with people, as well as with business systems and computers. Because many important financial decisions are made on the basis of accounting statements and services, you should have high standards and lots of integrity.

Salaries

Most people working in accounting and auditing make a decent salary. Some, especially those who are employed year-round by large corporations, may have more secure jobs with steady paychecks, although others, working for themselves in a consulting capacity, can do quite well. In general, the average salary of accountants and auditors is about $50,800. The middle half of those working earn between $39,890 and $66,900, the top 10 percent of accountants and auditors earn more than $88,610, and the bottom 10 percent earn less than $32,320. In the federal government, one of the largest employers of accountants and auditors, the starting annual salary for junior accountants and auditors is about $24,700. If you have a superior academic record, you might start at $30,600, while applicants with a master's degree or two years of professional experience usually began at $37,400. According to the Bureau of Labor Statistics, the median annual earnings in the industries employing the largest numbers of accountants and auditors are as follows:

Federal executive branch and U.S. Postal Service	$56,900
Accounting, tax preparation, bookkeeping, and payroll services	$53,870
Management of companies and enterprises	$52,260
Local government	$47,440
State government	$43,400

According to a salary survey conducted by the National Association of Colleges and Employers (www.naceweb.org), bachelor's degree candidates in accounting received starting offers averaging $43,269 a year in 2005, while master's degree candidates in accounting were offered $46,251 initially. According to a 2005 salary survey conducted by Robert Half International (www.rhi .com), a staffing services firm specializing in accounting and finance, accountants and auditors with up to one year of experience earned between $28,250 and $45,000 a year. Those with one to three years of experience earned between $33,000 and $52,000. Senior accountants and auditors earned between $40,750 and $69,750, managers between $48,000 and $90,000, and directors of accounting and auditing between $64,750 and $200,750. The wide range in salaries is due to the different kinds of companies for which you could work, locations (big cities versus small towns), and levels of education and professional credentials you could possess, all of which influence the amount of pay you receive.

Working for the IRS

The IRS (www.irs.gov), an agency of the Treasury Department, is one of the single largest employers of accountants in the United States. Under the national office, regional offices are responsible for overseeing the various district offices located in each state. The number of district offices in each state depends on the population—states with higher populations require more offices. Each district office is further divided into divisions, such as the Examination Division, the Collections Division, and the Criminal Investigation Division. Each division is then divided into branches, and each branch is made up of several groups. The group is the basic unit of the branch where the revenue agents, collection officers, or criminal investigation agents belong.

Once a person is hired as an Internal Revenue Agent, the IRS trains the new employee. The training consists of five phases, and each phase is divided into two types of training: classroom and on-the-job. During the classroom training, the agents learn tax law and must take and pass tests. During the on-the-job training, the new agent conducts examinations under the guidance of an on-the-job instructor, who is usually an experienced agent. The total amount of time to complete these phases is about two to three years; however, the first year of employment with the IRS is conditional. This means that if an agent does not pass the first two phases of training, he or she may be fired. After the first year, if the agent has passed all training during that year, the job becomes a career, or permanent, job.

An audit of a tax return, whether it is a return of an individual or a business, is not just auditing the books and records of the person. An audit includes reviewing the financial status or economic situation of the person or business. This means that the examiner (agent) must evaluate the facts and circumstances of each case to determine if what is reported on the return is credible or not. For example, if a company has been reporting losses for a few years, the agents wonder how the company manages to survive. Is someone loaning money or capital to this company? Do the shareholders contribute more capital? Does the company get loans from financial institutions?

If the answers to those questions are no, then it's unlikely that the company is incurring losses every year because they would not have enough money to continue to function. Think of audits as numerical investigations, with the agent as the sleuth, trying to determine the truth of the matter.

The following are the general tasks or activities of an IRS agent:

- **Establish workload priorities.** Plan the examinations and schedule appointments required to conduct the examinations.
- **Apply accounting procedures.** Gain an understanding of the taxpayer's accounting practices and bookkeeping systems. Reconcile amounts on the returns to the books and records and analyze the relationship between the income statements and the balance sheets in order to identify potential issues. Determine the quality of the internal control of the company through interviews with the people involved in the business, employees, and/or accountants. After assessing the control structure, select the audit techniques to use.
- **Identify issues.** Review the returns and internal control of the company to determine which items have significant tax potential.
- **Find the facts.** Gather evidence to resolve the tax issues identified and support the conclusions reached. Evaluate the credibility of all evidence obtained.
- **Apply tax laws.** Conduct research to understand and clarify the tax law applicable to the person or business. Apply the Internal Revenue Code, regulations, rulings, court cases, and so forth, to the individual's facts to decide issues and arrive at the correct tax determination.
- **Fill out paperwork.** Prepare papers that reflect the audit steps taken and that support the conclusions reached.

Prepare accurate examination reports, schedules, and forms. Assemble the case file to close the case.

- **Practice good customer relations.** Conduct discussions both inside and outside the office in a professional manner.

The IRS allows its field employees (field employees are revenue agents, collections officers, and anyone whose job requires that they go out of their offices in order to perform their duties) to work out of their homes. However, most field employees are expected to work in the field at least 50 to 80 percent of their time. A revenue agent, for example, would have duties involving auditing corporations and partnerships, so his or her time would mostly be spent doing the examinations at the places of business or at the offices of the accountants that represent these entities. A trip to the office is necessary only when there is a meeting, to do monthly reports, to pick up mail, to get cases, to submit cases, and to do research.

One of the benefits of this type of job is its flexibility in terms of the office or work hours. IRS employees may start work at any time between 7:00 and 9:00 A.M. and finish the day any time between 3:30 and 5:30 P.M. Agents do not have to take work home with them. This means that they work eight hours a day and the rest of the time is their own—compared to accountants who work for private firms and who, at times, have to work overtime whether they want to or not. Employees may work part-time or work extra hours in order to take time off when needed at other times during the year.

Actuaries

Why do young drivers pay more for automobile insurance than older drivers? How much should an insurance policy cost? How much should an organization contribute each year to its pension fund? Actuaries, who help businesses create and maintain insurance and pension plans, provide answers to these and similar questions. In addition, actuaries assemble and analyze statistics to calculate probabilities of death, sickness, injury, disability, unemployment, retirement, and property loss. They use this information to determine the expected insured loss. For example, they may calculate the probability of claims due to automobile accidents, which can vary depending on the insured's driving history, type of car, and other factors. Actuaries must make sure that the price charged for the insurance will enable the company to pay all claims and expenses as they occur. Finally, this price must be profitable and yet be competitive with other insurance companies. In a similar manner, the actuary calculates premium rates and determines policy contract provisions for each type of insurance offered. Most actuaries specialize in life, health, or property and casualty insurance; others specialize in pension plans or in financial planning and investment.

Actuaries focus on a variety of specific issues, depending on where they work. For example, actuaries in executive positions help determine company policy. In that role, they may be called upon to explain complex technical matters to other company executives, government officials, policyholders, and the public. They may testify before public agencies on proposed legislation affecting the insurance business, for example, or explain changes in premium rates or contract provisions. They also may help companies develop plans to enter new lines of business, such as environmental risk or long-term health care. The small number of actuaries who work for the federal government usually deal with a particular insurance or pension program, such as Social Security or life insurance for veterans and members of the armed forces. Actuaries in state government are usually employed by state insurance departments that regulate insurance companies, oversee the operations of state retirement or pension systems, handle unemployment insurance or workers' compensation problems, and assess the impact of proposed legislation. They might determine whether the rates charged by an insurance company are proper or whether an employee benefit plan is financially sound.

Most actuaries either work in pricing or reserving departments of insurance companies. The pricing actuaries are the people who help determine how much an insured person or company pays in premiums for an insurance policy. Actuaries working in the reserving departments of insurance companies make sure that a company has set adequate reserves to fund future payments to those who make claims on their insurance policies. The National Council on Compensation Insurance (NCCI; www.ncci.com) is the administrator of many state workers' compensation market pools—a collection of companies that pool money that will go to workers who get hurt on the job. All insurers in a state are required to participate in these pools, which help distribute the amount of risk among different kinds of businesses. Thus, no one business will be hit harder than any other with payments to employees who get hurt on the job and can't continue to work. Reserve actuaries predict how much loss will develop in these pools, so the participating insurance companies can set their reserve rates.

Numbers are the lifeblood of an actuary's work. They spend the majority of their time analyzing historical data and gathering information about current and expected future trends that will impact an insurer. Frequently, they use computer applications to assist them in their analyses.

Actuaries must be aware of the quickly changing insurance environment both within a company and in the whole insurance industry. Actuaries are actively involved in making critical decisions that have a direct impact on the financial stability of a company, so they must be well informed in their areas of expertise. They may also be required to make presentations to others within the company or to clients in order to explain laws and actuarial processes, so they should have the ability to communicate complex topics to those who aren't familiar with the ins and outs of actuarial work.

Consulting is another area to consider if you are the type who likes to be your own boss. Consulting actuaries provide advice for a fee to various clients, including insurance companies, corporations, hospitals, labor unions, government agencies, and attorneys. Some consulting actuaries set up pension and welfare plans, calculate future benefits, and determine the amount of employer contributions. They also provide advice to health care and financial services firms. Consultants may be called upon to testify in court regarding the value of potential lifetime earnings lost by a person who has been disabled or killed in an accident, the current value of future pension benefits in divorce cases, or the calculation of automobile insurance rates.

So where do actuaries work and what are the hours like? Well, the majority of time on the job for actuaries is spent in the office working at a desk, although some actuaries, particularly consultants, travel to meet with clients. This job doesn't require any physical activity, and the offices in which you would work are generally comfortable and pleasant. Most actuaries work at least forty hours a week; consulting actuaries may be required to work more than forty hours per week, and the more they work, the more money they can make.

Job Outlook

According to government statistics, actuaries hold about eighteen thousand jobs, and about six out of ten are employed by the insurance industry. A growing number of actuaries work for firms that provide a range of corporate services, especially management and public relations, or for firms offering consulting services. A relatively small number of actuaries are employed by security and commodity brokers or by government agencies.

The outlook is good for actuaries. The government expects the employment of actuaries to grow faster than the average for all occupations through the year 2014. For the time being, employment opportunities should remain good for those who qualify for jobs because the difficult examination system restricts the number of candidates. The insurance industry, the largest employer of actuaries, produces a steady demand for actuaries to develop, price, and evaluate a variety of insurance products and calculate the costs of new risks. New opportunities for actuaries are becoming available in the health care field as health care issues and Medicare reform receive growing attention. Increased regulation of managed health care companies and the desire to contain health care costs should continue to provide job opportunities for actuaries, who are needed to evaluate the risks associated with new medical issues, such as genetic testing and the impact of new diseases. Others in this field are involved in drafting health care legislation. Another growing area to consider is consulting. A significant number of new actuaries will find employment with consulting firms; companies that don't want to hire full-time actuaries often hire consultants to analyze various risks.

There are several ways to increase your chances of getting the best jobs, especially if you are a recent graduate from college. The best prospects for entry-level positions are for those who have passed at least one or two of the initial actuarial exams. Excellent computer skills are useful for getting jobs in just about any field, but it's particularly important in actuarial work, in which much of your time is spent working with computers in some fashion. Most jobs are found in cities, so you'll increase your chances of getting a job by moving to a place with a large population and numerous types of businesses. In particular, some states, such as Illinois, New Jersey, New York, and Connecticut, have high numbers of these jobs.

Training and Education

As you might expect, math plays a large part in the education and training of an actuary. A bachelor's degree in mathematics or a business-related discipline, such as actuarial science, statistics, economics, finance, or accounting, is the best educational background for a landing a beginning job in a large life or casualty insurance company. Only about fifty-five colleges and universities offer an actuarial science program, although hundreds of schools offer degrees in mathematics or statistics. Courses in accounting, computer science, and insurance are particularly useful, so be sure to take these types of classes in high school to give you a head start. Finally, some companies hire job seekers with a liberal arts degree, provided you have a working knowledge of mathematics, including calculus, probability, and statistics, and have demonstrated this ability by passing at least the beginning actuarial exams required for professional designation.

Taking and passing actuarial exams is key to your success in this field; it's advantageous to pass two or more of the examinations offered by professional actuarial societies while still in college. These exams are given by three societies that sponsor programs leading to full professional status in their specialties. The Society of Actuaries (www.soa.org) gives a series of actuarial examinations for the life and health insurance, pension, and finance and investment fields, and the Casualty Actuarial Society (www.casact.org) gives a series of examinations for property and casualty issues. Exams test your abilities and knowledge of linear algebra, probability, calculus, statistics, risk theory, and actuarial mathematics. The first few examinations help students evaluate their potential as actuaries. Higher starting salaries are just one benefit of going through the stress of taking these exams.

Passing examinations is critical to professional advancement and necessary for membership in one of the actuarial societies, yet the examination process can seem overwhelming, requiring many study hours outside of work. Even the brightest actuarial candidate needs five to ten years to complete the entire series of examinations. Fortunately, most employers provide salary increases and/or promotions with each passed examination. Most employers also offer study programs that allow actuaries to take study time at work to prepare for their actuarial examinations.

When you're first starting out, you may rotate among jobs to learn various actuarial skills and different phases of insurance work, such as marketing, underwriting, or product development. Job duties include the somewhat tedious work of preparing data for actuarial tables or performing other simple tasks. As you gain experience, however, you will supervise clerks, prepare correspondence and reports, and conduct research. In addition, keep in mind that many companies offer summer internship programs. This experience may help you decide if actuarial science is a career you want to pursue, and it may lead to a full-time position after college.

Salaries

Because companies value their skills and services, actuaries tend to earn good money for their work. In fact, Challenger, Gray & Christmas, an international outplacement firm, recently declared actuarial jobs as one of the highest-paying jobs in the United States and the *Wall Street Journal* ranked it as one of the best jobs to have. According to the U.S. Department of Labor, the median annual earnings of actuaries are $76,300. The middle 50 percent of these workers earn between $54,800 and $107,700. According to the National Association of Colleges and Employers (www .naceweb.org), the starting salary for new graduates with a bachelor's degree in actuarial science averages about $52,700 a year. In addition, insurance companies and consulting firms often give merit increases to actuaries as they gain experience, and some companies also offer cash bonuses for each professional designation achieved. Actuaries typically receive benefits in addition to their salaries, including vacation and sick leave, health and life insurance, and pension plans.

For More Information

For more information about actuarial careers, check out the Be an Actuary website (www.beanactuary.org), which is cosponsored by the Society of Actuaries and the Casualty Society of Actuaries. This website is packed with useful information for people of all ages interested in actuarial jobs, including videos of people working as actuaries talking about their work, a newsletter about the future of the field, information about the state of the current job market, and special sections for students, including an interactive actuarial exam for high school and college students.

Statisticians

Statistics is the scientific application of mathematical principles to the collection, analysis, and presentation of numerical data. Statisticians contribute to scientific inquiry by applying their mathematical and statistical knowledge to the design of surveys and experiments; the collection, processing, and analysis of data; and the interpretation of the results. Statisticians apply their numerical knowledge to a variety of subject areas, such as biology, economics, engineering, medicine, public health, psychology, marketing, education, and even sports! For example, they may use statistical techniques to predict population growth or economic conditions, develop quality-control tests for manufactured products, assess the nature of environmental problems, analyze legal and social problems, or help business managers and government officials make decisions and evaluate the results of new programs. Because statistics are used in so many areas, it is sometimes difficult to distinguish statisticians from specialists in other fields who use statistics. For example, a statistician working with data on economic conditions may have the title of economist.

Often statisticians are able to obtain information about a group of people or things by surveying a small portion, called a sample, of the group. For example, to determine the size of the total audience for particular programs, television rating services ask only a few thousand families, rather than all viewers, which programs they watch. Statisticians decide where and how to gather the data, determine the type and size of the sample group, and develop the survey questionnaire or reporting form. They also prepare instructions for the workers who collect and tabulate the data. Statisticians use computers extensively to process large amounts of data for statistical modeling and graphic analysis.

In business and industry, statisticians play an important role in quality control and in product development and improvement. Similarly, at a computer software firm, statisticians might help construct new statistical software packages to analyze data more accurately and efficiently. In addition to product development and testing, some statisticians also are involved in deciding what products a company should manufacture, how much to charge for them, and to whom the products should be marketed. They may also determine the risks and returns of certain investments.

Job Outlook

According to government statistics, statisticians hold about nineteen thousand jobs in the United States. Twenty percent of these jobs are with the federal government, where statisticians are concentrated in the Departments of Commerce, Agriculture, and Health and Human Services. Another 20 percent work for state and local governments, including state colleges and universities. Most of the remaining jobs are in private industry, especially in scientific research and development services, insurance carriers, and pharmaceutical manufacturing. In addition, many professionals with a background in statistics are among the fifty-three thousand postsecondary mathematical science teachers.

Career projections for statisticians are difficult to locate and interpret because, while employment of statisticians is projected to grow more slowly than average for all occupations throughout 2014, many jobs that require a degree in statistics do not carry the title statistician. Despite slow growth projection, opportunities should remain favorable for those with statistics degrees.

The use of statistics is widespread and growing. Among graduates with master's degrees in statistics, those with a strong background in an allied field, such as health care, should have the best prospects of finding jobs related to their field of study. Federal agencies will hire statisticians in many fields, including demography, agriculture, consumer and producer surveys, and environmental quality. Because the federal government is one of the few employers that considers a bachelor's degree an adequate entry-level qualification, competition for entry-level positions with the government is expected to be strong for persons just meeting the minimum qualifications for statisticians.

A range of industries and fields employ statisticians; no matter what your interests are, you can combine them with statistics. For example, private industry, in the face of increasing competition and strong government regulation, requires statisticians, especially at the master's and doctoral degree levels, to not only monitor but improve productivity and quality in the manufacture of various products, including pharmaceuticals, motor vehicles, chemicals, and food products. Pharmaceutical firms need more statisticians to assess the safety and effectiveness of the rapidly expanding number of drugs. To meet growing competition, motor vehicle manufacturers will need statisticians to monitor the quality of automobiles, trucks, and their components. Statisticians with knowledge of engineering and the physical sciences may find jobs in research and development, working with scientists and engineers to help improve design and production processes in order to ensure consistent quality of newly developed products. Business firms may rely more heavily than in the past on workers with a background in statistics to forecast sales, analyze business conditions, and help solve management problems. In addition, sophisticated statistical services will increasingly be contracted out to consulting firms.

Training and Education

Approximately 230 universities offer degree programs in statistics, biostatistics, or mathematics. Many other colleges and universities offer graduate-level courses in applied statistics. Acceptance into graduate statistics programs does not require an undergraduate degree in statistics, although good training in mathematics is essential.

Although employment opportunities exist for individuals with a bachelor's degree, in particular with the federal government, a master's degree in statistics or mathematics is usually the minimum educational requirement for most jobs. Research and academic positions in institutions of higher education require at least a master's degree, and usually a doctorate, in statistics. Beginning positions in industrial research often require a master's degree combined with several years of experience.

Required statistical subjects include differential and integral calculus, statistical methods, mathematical modeling, and probability theory. Additional courses that undergraduates should take include linear algebra, design and analysis of experiments, applied multivariate analysis, and mathematical statistics.

Because computers are used extensively in this field, you must have a strong background in computer science. For positions involving quality and productivity improvement, training in engineering is also useful. Courses in economics and business administration are helpful for many jobs in market research, business analysis, and forecasting. Finally, good communication skills are important for statisticians in industry, who often need to explain technical matters to persons without statistical expertise. An understanding of business and the economy also is valuable for those who plan to work in private industry.

Salaries

Statisticians command a range of salaries. According to the U.S. Department of Labor, the median annual earnings of statisticians are about $58,600. Of those working in all areas and holding a spectrum of degrees, the middle 50 percent earn between $42,800 and $80,900; the lowest 10 percent earn less than $32,900; and the highest 10 percent earn more than $100,500. The average annual salary for those working for the federal government in nonsupervisory, supervisory, and managerial positions is about $81,300, while mathematical statisticians average $91,500. According to a 2005 survey by the National Association of Colleges and Employers, starting salary offers for statistics graduates with a bachelor's degree averaged $43,500 a year. Benefits for statisticians are similar to those for other professionals who work in an office setting; vacation and sick leave, health and life insurance, and a retirement plan are common.

Additional Jobs

The jobs featured in this chapter are only a few of the many different kinds of number-crunching jobs available to you. Teaching math at all levels, including grade school, junior high, high school, and college, is another option for those with a head for figures. Small-business owners must have a strong knowledge of numbers in order to make sure their businesses run profitably. Finally, if you don't relish the risks involved in running your own business, you can examine profit margins for large companies working in the finance department. Look around you and ask those you meet about their jobs; you might be surprised to find there are lots of possibilities for perfectionists who like working with numbers.

CHAPTER THREE

Lawyers

T he legal system affects nearly every aspect of our society, from buying a home to crossing the street. Lawyers form the backbone of this vital system and hold positions of great responsibility in our society. Lawyers help uphold the law, and they are very necessary to the smooth functioning of our society.

Lawyers, also called attorneys, act as both advocates and advisors. As advocates, they represent one of the parties in criminal and civil trials by presenting evidence and arguing in court to support their clients. As advisors, lawyers counsel their clients concerning their legal rights and obligations and suggest particular courses of action in business and personal matters. Whether acting as an advocate or an advisor, all attorneys research the intent of laws and judicial decisions and apply the law to the specific circumstances faced by their clients; this is where their perfectionism comes in. In order to be effective at their jobs, lawyers must give accurate and reliable advice in a timely fashion. They must have excellent and accurate memory recall in order to present their case. There is no room for error in this perfectionist profession.

Most lawyers are in private practice, concentrating on criminal or civil law. In criminal law, lawyers represent individuals who have been charged with crimes and argue their cases in courts of law. Attorneys dealing with civil law assist clients with litigation, wills, trusts, contracts, mortgages, titles, and leases. Other lawyers handle only public-interest cases—civil or criminal—that may have an impact on whole communities, not just one client.

....

Areas of Specialty

The more detailed aspects of a lawyer's job depend upon his or her field of specialization and position. Although all lawyers are licensed to represent parties in court, some appear in court more frequently than others. For example, trial lawyers spend significantly more time in court than in-house lawyers. Still, even trial lawyers spend the majority of their time outside the courtroom conducting research, interviewing clients and witnesses, and handling other details in preparation for a trial.

Lawyers may specialize in a number of areas, such as bankruptcy, probate, international, or elder law. Those specializing in environmental law, for example, may represent interest groups, waste disposal companies, or construction firms in their dealings with the U.S. Environmental Protection Agency (EPA) and other federal and state agencies. These lawyers help clients prepare and file for licenses and applications for approval before certain activities may occur. In addition, they represent clients' interests in administrative adjudications. Some lawyers specialize in the growing field of intellectual property, helping to protect clients' claims to copyrights, artwork under contract, product designs, and computer programs. Still other lawyers advise insurance companies about the legality of insurance transactions, guiding the company in writing insurance policies to conform with the law and to protect the companies from unwarranted claims. When claims are filed against insurance companies, these attorneys review the claims and represent the companies in court. No matter what your area of specialization, firsthand experience with the operation of that field of work provides a tremendous advantage in the legal profession.

At some institutions, lawyers don't have rigidly defined areas of specialization, so each might work on a wide variety of projects. The areas of law that might be involved include: employment, employee benefits, contract, commercial, intellectual property, banking, general corporate, antitrust, environmental, safety, technology, tax, litigation, or just about anything else. Lawyers might also monitor pending federal and state legislation that affects the industry.

Criminal Lawyers

In criminal law, lawyers represent individuals who have been charged with crimes and argue their cases in courts of law. Lawyers who specialize in trial work must possess the ability to think quickly, be able to speak with ease and authority, and be thoroughly familiar with courtroom rules and strategy. As a criminal lawyer, you might work in private practice, which means that people charged with crimes hire you to defend them, or you may work for the city as a public defender and be assigned to defend people who cannot afford their own lawyer. If you choose to work in this area, you should know that you may be hired to defend people who are indeed guilty of the crimes for which they have been charged; this can be a significant source of conflict for some people.

Civil Lawyers

In civil law, attorneys assist clients with litigation, wills, trusts, contracts, mortgages, titles, and leases. Some manage property as trustee or, as executor, see that provisions of a client's will are carried out. Other lawyers handle only public-interest cases, either civil or criminal, that have a potential impact extending well beyond the individual client. Still others work for legal aid societies, which are private, nonprofit organizations established to serve disadvantaged people. These lawyers generally handle civil rather than criminal cases. Some other specializations within civil law include:

- bankruptcy
- probate
- international law
- environmental law

- intellectual property
- insurance law
- family law
- real estate law
- public defense

House Counsel

Lawyers are sometimes employed full-time by a single client. If the client is a corporation, the lawyer is known as "house counsel" and usually advises the company concerning legal issues related to its business activities. These issues might involve patents, government regulations, contracts with other companies, property interests, or collective-bargaining agreements with unions.

In-house counsels can be found everywhere. For example, you could work as a lawyer for a Federal Reserve bank, one of the operating arms of the national Federal Reserve System that carry out various system functions, including operating a nationwide payments system, distributing currency and coin, supervising and regulating member banks and bank holding companies, and serving as banker for the U.S. Treasury. A typical day working as this kind of lawyer usually involves some combination of meetings, client counseling, research, writing, planning, public speaking, telephone calls, traveling, and administrative duties. You might also attend continuing legal education seminars from time to time and serve on business-related committees and task forces.

If you were an in-house lawyer working for a publishing company, for example, you might help your company, through careful planning, anticipate legal problems and make practical decisions. You would spend time drafting contracts and reviewing manuscripts. On the other hand, you could serve as legal counsel representing writers and publishers who need assistance with their publishing contracts or their collaboration or work-for-hire agreements.

Government Attorneys

Attorneys are employed at various levels of government. Lawyers working for state attorneys general, prosecutors, public defenders, and courts play a key role in the criminal justice system. At the federal level, attorneys investigate cases for the Department of Justice or other agencies. Also, lawyers at every government level help develop programs, draft laws, interpret legislation, establish enforcement procedures, and argue civil and criminal cases on behalf of the government.

Intellectual Property Lawyers

Valuable intellectual property generally does not suddenly or magically appear; the best business ideas are often the product of careful research and development. Indeed, artistic and literary creations frequently result from months and years of creative effort. That's where intellectual property lawyers come in. These lawyers work to ensure that those who have come up with a new idea or product are protected from having others steal or copy them. The law recognizes four main types of intellectual property: patents, copyrights, trademarks, and trade secrets.

Where there is creativity or innovation, there is a need for intellectual property lawyers. Their clients are generally creative types, and their services are in demand across the United States and around the world. If you choose this specialty, you're sure to find plenty of interesting and exciting work available no matter where you choose to live.

Law Clerks

Law clerks are fully trained attorneys who choose to work with a judge or another lawyer, either for a one- to two-year stint out of law school or as a full-time, professional career. Their duties involve doing research, writing reports, and summarizing information. They check facts of cases and make sure the arguments are valid, and they may deliver subpoenas to witnesses who are needed to testify about certain facts. Law clerks who work for lawyers are usually doing an internship, which gives them a chance to sample various parts of the job before they become lawyers. Some law clerks do almost everything a lawyer does; however, since they have not taken the state bar exam, they are unable to officially appear in court. Depending on the state, there may be other duties that law clerks cannot fulfill.

Law Professors

A relatively small number of trained attorneys work in law schools. Most are faculty members who specialize in one or more subjects; others serve as administrators. Some work full-time in nonacademic settings and teach part-time. You need to have a Ph.D. to pursue this job, and you must enjoy working with students. You may have to move frequently in order to gain tenure status at a college or university. In addition, many schools want their professors to publish articles or books in order to increase the prestige of the law school program. If you think you might enjoy passing your expertise on to others, then this might be the career for you.

Work Settings and Hours

Where can you find these upholders of the law? Lawyers do most of their work in offices, law libraries, and courtrooms, although they sometimes meet in clients' homes or places of business and, when necessary, in hospitals or prisons. They frequently travel to attend meetings, to gather evidence, and to appear before courts, legislative bodies, and other authorities. Salaried lawyers in government and private corporations generally have structured work schedules. Lawyers in private practice may work irregular hours while conducting research, conferring with clients, or preparing briefs. Indeed, lawyers often work long hours; about half regularly work fifty hours or more per week. They are under particularly heavy pressure, for example, when a case is being tried. Preparation for court includes keeping abreast of the latest laws and judicial decisions.

No matter the setting, whether acting as advocate or prosecutor, all attorneys interpret the law and apply it to specific situations, a task that requires strong research and communication abilities. Lawyers perform in-depth research into the purposes behind the applicable laws and into judicial decisions that have been applied under circumstances similar to those currently faced by the client. While all lawyers continue to make use of law libraries to prepare cases, some supplement conventional printed sources with computer databases in order to search the legal literature and identify texts that may be relevant to a specific subject. In litigation that involves many supporting documents, lawyers use computers to organize and index the material. They then communicate to others the information obtained by research.

There are some downsides to working as a lawyer. This is a high-pressure, high-stress field; lawyers must give accurate legal advice, often within a very short time frame. You're probably familiar with lawyer jokes and the bad rap lawyers have been given as being shifty or untrustworthy. While there are some bad apples in the legal profession, as in all professions, most lawyers place a high value on ethical behavior and client service. Billing clients is a necessary, although dull, bookkeeping task that lawyers have to perform in order to get paid. You must keep track of the hours you spend working for each client in order to bill them since legal work is rarely, if ever, done on a flat-fee basis.

Job Outlook

According to government statistics, job growth for lawyers is steady. For the most part, job growth will result from increasing demand for legal services in such areas as health care, intellectual property, venture capital, energy, elder, antitrust, and environmental law. In addition, the wider availability and affordability of legal clinics should result in increased use of legal services by middle-income people. However, growth in demand for lawyers may be limited as businesses, in an effort to reduce costs, increasingly use large accounting firms and paralegals to perform some of the same functions that lawyers do. For example, accounting firms may provide employee-benefit counseling, process documents, or handle various other services previously performed by a law firm. Also, mediation and dispute resolution increasingly are being used as alternatives to litigation.

The time when you'll face the most competition for job openings is when you graduate from law school. As previously mentioned, graduates from highly regarded law schools with superior academic records will have the best job opportunities. Also, lawyers are increasingly finding work in nontraditional areas for which legal training is an asset, but not normally a requirement—for example, administrative, managerial, and business positions in banks, insurance firms, real estate companies, government agencies, and other organizations. Some graduates may even have to accept positions in areas outside of their field of interest or for which they feel overqualified. Some recent law school graduates unable to find permanent positions are turning to temporary staffing firms that place attorneys in short-term jobs until they are able to secure full-time positions. This service allows companies to hire lawyers on an as-needed basis and permits beginning lawyers to develop practical skills while looking for permanent positions. Because of the keen competition for jobs, your willingness to relocate may be an advantage. In addition, employers are increasingly seeking graduates who have advanced law degrees and experience in a specialty, such as tax, patent, or admiralty law.

Salaried jobs are growing in number as businesses and all levels of government employ more and more staff attorneys. Most salaried positions are in urban areas where government agencies, law firms, and big corporations are concentrated. The number of self-employed lawyers is expected to decrease slowly, reflecting the difficulty of establishing a profitable new practice in the face of competition from larger, established law firms. In addition, the growing complexity of law, which encourages specialization, along with the cost of maintaining up-to-date legal research materials, favors larger firms. If, however, you have your heart set on establishing your own practice, this will probably be easiest to accomplish in small towns and expanding suburban areas. In these types of communities, there is less competition from large, corporate law firms.

Training and Education

Grades are especially important for those going to law school. The market for new lawyers is tight, and those with low grades will have more trouble getting a job than those with high grades. Law school is tough, too, so be prepared to study—a lot! Before seriously considering this career, be honest with yourself and ask yourself the following questions: Do you enjoy learning? Are you a dedicated student? Do you like history? Are you a persuasive arguer? If you answered yes to the majority of these questions, then you have the potential to succeed in law school.

The American Bar Association (ABA) provides information on each of the 191 law schools it has approved, state requirements for admission to legal practice, a directory of state bar examination administrators, and other information on legal education. Information on the bar examination, financial aid for law students, and law as a career may also be obtained from the ABA website at www.aba.org.

To practice law in the courts of any state or other jurisdiction, a person must be licensed, or admitted to its bar, under rules established by the jurisdiction's highest court. Virtually every state requires that applicants for admission to the bar pass a written bar examination. Most jurisdictions also require applicants to pass a separate written ethics examination.

Lawyers who have been admitted to the bar in one jurisdiction occasionally may be admitted to the bar in another without taking an examination if they meet that jurisdiction's standards of good moral character and have a specified period of legal experience. Federal courts and agencies set their own qualifications for those practicing before them.

To qualify for the bar examination in most states, an applicant must complete at least three years of college and graduate from a law school approved by the ABA or the proper state authorities. (ABA approval signifies that the law school, particularly its library and faculty, meets certain standards developed by the association to promote quality legal education.) The required college and law school education usually takes seven years of full-time study after high school: four years of undergraduate study, followed by three years in law school. Although some law schools accept a very small number of students after three years of college, most require applicants to have a bachelor's degree. To meet the needs of students who can only attend part-time, a number of law schools offer night or part-time divisions that usually require four years of study.

There really is no recommended prelaw major, although prospective lawyers should develop proficiency in writing, speaking, reading, researching, analyzing, and thinking logically—skills needed to succeed both in law school and in the profession. Regardless of the major you choose, you should have a broad, multidisciplinary background. Courses in English, foreign languages, public speaking, government, philosophy, history, economics, mathematics, and computer science, among others, are most useful.

Students interested in particular aspects of law may find related courses helpful. For example, prospective patent lawyers need a strong background in engineering or science, and future tax lawyers must have extensive knowledge of accounting.

Acceptance by most law schools depends on the applicant's ability to demonstrate an aptitude for the study of law, usually through good undergraduate grades, the Law School Admission Test (LSAT), the quality of the applicant's undergraduate school, any prior work experience, and sometimes a personal interview. However, law schools vary in the weight they place on each of these factors. All law schools approved by the ABA require that applicants take the LSAT. Nearly all law schools require that applicants have certified transcripts sent to the Law School Data Assembly Service. This service then sends applicants' LSAT scores and their standardized records of college grades to the law schools of their choice. Both this service and the LSAT are administered by the Law School Admission Counsel (www.lsac.org).

Graduates receive the degree of juris doctor (J.D.) or bachelor of law (LL.B.) as the first professional degree. Advanced law degrees may be desirable for those planning to specialize, do research, or teach. Some law students pursue joint degree programs, which generally require an additional year. Joint degrees are offered in a number of areas, including law and business administration and law and public administration.

Salaries

Contrary to the experience of John Grisham's hero in *The Firm*, annual salaries of beginning lawyers in private industry average about $55,000, although top graduates from the nation's best law schools can start at over $80,000 a year. Annual starting salaries for attorneys range from about $40,000 to $80,000, depending upon academic and personal qualifications. Other factors affecting the salaries offered to new graduates include academic record; type, size, and location of employer; and the specialized educational background desired. Those in private practice and working for businesses earn more than those working for the government.

Salaries of experienced attorneys also vary widely according to the type, size, and location of the employer. The average salary of the most experienced lawyers in private industry runs about $95,000, but some senior lawyers who are partners in the nation's top law firms can earn over $1 million.

Salaried lawyers receive increases as they assume greater responsibility. Lawyers starting a private practice may need to work part-time in other occupations during the early years to supplement their incomes. Their incomes usually grow as their practices develop. Lawyers who are partners in law firms generally earn more than those who practice alone.

Research the Possibilities

If you're the type of perfectionist who likes to work and study hard, then a career in law might be a perfect fit for you. This is an area that demands hard work but can provide high pay and job satisfaction as compensation. Ask lawyers in your community if you can speak with them about their jobs or spend some time in court watching proceedings to better understand what the job is really like. Preparation and research, which are keys to success in law, will be the key to discovering whether or not this job is right for you.

Architects

W hen you're next out and about in the city or town in which you live, look around you. Check out all the buildings, houses, museums, and parks you visit or know. Pay particular attention to those you find attractive or interesting and try to identify specifically what it is that's interesting to you. Is it the shapes of the windows or the height of the structure? Is it the large, graceful wraparound porch or the fountains and sculpted gardens surrounding the curving walkways? Architects of various persuasions are the minds behind these magnificent and interesting gardens and buildings that you're admiring.

Architects are creative forces who shape the way our worlds look. They design everything from the interiors of houses and offices to buildings large and small to outdoor amphitheaters to gardens and parks. The possibilities of their work are almost limitless.

Most architects specialize in one kind of work, such as the design of one type of building—hospitals, schools, or houses, for example. Historical architecture, or restoration architecture, as it is also called, involves the meticulous work of returning a building to its former appearance at a particular period in history. Landscape architecture is the design of outside areas that are beautiful, functional, and compatible with the natural environment. A landscape architect can work with small residential or commercial projects, or with complex projects on a much larger scale. These could include projects for cities or counties, industrial parks, historical sites, and a variety of other settings. Industrial architects design factories and other areas meant for the production of goods.

No matter what the area of specialty, however, an architect's work must be accurate and precise in order to result in structures that are safe and can withstand the test of time. Extreme examples of precision in architecture are gravity-defying skyscrapers, such as the Sears Tower in Chicago, or structures constructed along earthquake fault lines. Architecture is, indeed, a suitable career for perfectionists.

Building Architects

The design of a building involves far more than its appearance. Buildings must also be functional, safe, and economical and must suit the needs of the people who use them. Architects take all these things into consideration when they design buildings and other structures.

In the first step in the design process, the architect and client discuss the purposes, requirements, and budget of a project. Based on these discussions, the architect prepares a report specifying the design requirements. In some cases, the architect assists in conducting environmental impact analyses and selecting a site. The architect then prepares drawings and written information and presents his or her ideas to the client.

After the initial proposals are discussed and accepted, the architect develops the final construction plans. These plans show the building's appearance and details for its construction and include drawings of the structural system; air-conditioning, heating, and ventilating systems; electrical systems; plumbing systems; and possibly site and landscape plans. Architects also specify the building materials and, in some cases, the interior furnishings. In developing designs, architects follow building codes, zoning laws, fire regulations, and other ordinances, such as those that require easy access by disabled persons.

While architects have traditionally used pencil and paper to produce design and construction drawings, architects are increasingly turning to computer-aided design and drafting (CADD) technology for these important tasks. Typically, much of the precision work of the planning and design process is conducted using a computer, while the prototype of the building or other design space is a hand-constructed model or drawing, filled in with color. Often, these creations are themselves miniature works of art.

Some architects assist clients in obtaining construction bids, selecting a contractor, and negotiating the construction contract. As construction proceeds, the architect may visit the building site in order to ensure that the contractor is following the design, meeting the schedule, using the specified materials, and meeting the specified standards for the quality of work. The job is not complete until all construction is finished, required tests are made, and construction costs are paid.

Architects design a wide variety of buildings, such as office and apartment buildings, schools, churches, factories, hospitals, houses, and airport terminals. They also design multibuilding complexes, such as urban centers, college campuses, industrial parks, and entire communities. In addition to designing buildings, architects may advise on the selection of building sites, prepare cost analysis and land-use studies, and do long-range planning for land development.

Job Outlook

Internship opportunities for new architectural students are expected to be good over the next decade, but more students are graduating with architectural degrees, so you should expect some competition for entry-level jobs. Competition will be especially keen for jobs at the most prestigious architectural firms as prospective architects try to build their reputations. Prospective architects who have had internships while in school will have an advantage in obtaining intern positions after graduation. If you are able to distinguish yourself from others with your creativity and flare for design, then you shouldn't have a problem finding a good job in this field.

Employment of architects is strongly tied to the activity of the construction industry. Strong growth is expected to come from nonresidential construction, such as public buildings and stores. That doesn't mean that you shouldn't consider home building design if that's your area of interest. In fact, the government predicts that residential construction, buoyed by low interest rates, will also grow as more and more people become homeowners. If interest rates rise significantly, however, this sector may see a falloff in home building.

Current demographic trends also support an increase in demand for architects. As the population of states in the south and west continues to grow, the people living there will need new places to live and work. As the population continues to live longer and baby boomers begin to retire, the need for health care facilities, nursing homes, and retirement communities will grow. In education, buildings at all levels are getting older and class sizes are getting larger. This will require many school districts and universities to build new facilities and renovate existing ones.

Despite good overall job opportunities, some architects may not fare as well as others. The profession is geographically sensitive, and some parts of the country may have fewer new building projects than others. Also, many firms specialize in specific buildings, such as hospitals or office towers, and demand for these buildings may vary by region. Architects may find it increasingly necessary to gain reciprocity in order to compete for the best jobs and projects in other states. This means that moving and traveling may come with the job in the future.

Training and Education
Architects must be licensed or registered before they can contract to provide architectural services. This doesn't mean that you can't

work in the field if you aren't licensed. In fact, many architecture school graduates first start out working in architectural firms doing supportive work even though they are not licensed. However, a licensed architect is required to take legal responsibility for all the work produced by his or her office. There are three requirements, in general, that must be met in order to obtain licensure:

- a professional degree in architecture
- a period of practical training or internship (usually for three years)
- passage of all sections of the Architect Registration Examination

In most states, the professional degree must be from one of the approximately one hundred schools of architecture offering programs accredited by the National Architectural Accrediting Board. There are several types of professional degrees in architecture. More than half of all architecture degrees are from five-year bachelor of architecture programs intended for students entering from high school. Some schools offer a two-year master of architecture program for students with a preprofessional undergraduate degree in architecture or a related area, or a three- or four-year master of architecture program for students with a degree in another discipline. In addition, there are many combinations and variations of these degree programs.

The choice of degree type depends upon your preference and educational background. You should carefully consider the available options before committing to any program. For example, although the five-year bachelor of architecture program offers the fastest route to the professional degree, courses are specialized and, if you do not complete the program, moving to a nonarchitecture program may be difficult.

A typical program includes courses in architectural history and theory, building design—including technical and legal aspects—professional practice, math, physical sciences, and liberal arts.

Many architecture schools also offer graduate education for those who already have a bachelor's or master's degree in architecture or another discipline. Although graduate education beyond the professional degree is not essential for practicing architects, it is normally required for research, teaching, and certain specialties.

There are a variety of skills and talents you should possess in order to succeed in this field. Architects must be able to visually communicate their ideas to clients. Artistic and drawing ability is very helpful in doing this, but not essential. More important is a visual orientation and the ability to conceptualize and understand spatial relationships. Good communication skills (both written and oral), the ability to work independently or as part of a team, and creativity are important qualities for anyone interested in becoming an architect. Computer literacy is also required as most firms use computers for word processing, specifications writing, two- and three-dimensional drafting, and financial management. A knowledge of computer-aided design and drafting (CADD) is helpful and will become more important as architecture firms continue to adopt this technology.

During a training period leading up to licensure as architects, entry-level workers are called intern architects. This training period gives them practical work experience while they prepare for the Architect Registration Examination. Typical duties may include preparing construction drawings on CADD, assisting in the design of one part of a project, or managing the production of a small project.

New graduates usually begin in architecture firms, where they assist in preparing architectural documents or drawings. They also may do research on building codes and materials or write specifications for building materials, installation criteria, the quality of finishes, and other related details. Graduates with degrees in architecture may also enter related fields such as graphic, interior, or industrial design; urban planning; real estate development; civil engineering; or construction management.

Salaries

Unfortunately, you won't start out making a lot of money in this field. Someone fresh from graduate school can expect to earn about $30,000 per year, depending of course upon the size of the firm, the importance of the project, and the region of the country. Advancement would depend upon ability and accomplishments. The good news is that most firms offer paid internships for graduate students.

Salaries for architects, in general, however, are competitive with jobs in other fields. According to government statistics, the median annual earnings of all architects working in the United States are about $60,300. The middle 50 percent earn between $46,700 and $79,000. The lowest 10 percent earn less than $38,000, and the highest 10 percent earn more than $99,900. Granted, there is a wide span in the earnings described here. That's because the earnings of partners in established architectural firms may fluctuate due to changing business conditions. Some architects may also have difficulty establishing their own practices and may go through a period when expenses are greater than income, requiring substantial financial resources.

Restoration Architects

While you're looking around and paying attention to the various styles of architecture in your area, if you notice that you're more attracted to one style than another—the graceful, brightly painted Victorian homes or the clean lines and silhouettes of art deco buildings, for example—then you might be interested in becoming a restoration architect. A restoration architect, or an architect specializing in historic preservation, has experience similar to a general architect's: he or she understands how to plan spaces, how to organize construction materials, and how to put together construction documents. The difference between a general architect and a restoration architect is that the latter's work experience is primarily focused on historic buildings. In addition, the restoration architect has a specialized knowledge and understanding of federal, state, and local regulations with regard to historic preservation and is also aware of the standards set by the particular style of architecture.

In this line of work, you might be responsible for all sorts of properties—anything from small, privately owned residential-scale houses from the eighteenth century to nineteenth-century mansions designed in high style. In addition, you could work with historic commercial and industrial buildings from the nineteenth century, restoring them or practicing adaptive reuse, such as converting an old mill into an office building or a farmhouse into a meeting facility.

The following are the steps you might take when working on a project as a restoration architect:

1. Meet with the client and determine his or her goals for the property.
2. Analyze the existing conditions of the site, looking at the historical development of the building over time and taking photographs, field measurements, and written notes.
3. Develop a schematic plan, making preliminary drawings and sketches, and presenting the design to the client for approval. This stage could take four weeks or so.
4. Upon client approval of the project, produce an outline of the scope of work and come up with a cost estimate for the project.
5. Work on design development documents, which involves creating more detailed drawings and can take from six to eight weeks.
6. Produce construction documents over the next eight to twelve weeks, including drawings and specifications.
7. Develop construction specifications for bid requests and solicit cost estimates in order to select the best contractor to hire for this particular job.

8. Review construction plans with both the client and the contractor before any work actually begins.
9. Visit the site frequently in order to monitor the quality and progress of the work. Construction time varies but could take eight months to a year and a half depending upon the scope of the project.

After the construction is finished, you should have a happy client who is willing to recommend your services to others.

Training and Education

While this is a niche market, there are numerous training programs available for those interested in becoming a restoration architect. Both bachelor's and master's degree programs are available in this area. How much training you obtain is up to you, although having an advanced degree will make you more marketable in the field. In order to locate a school in your state that offers undergraduate or graduate programs in restoration architecture, visit the National Council for Preservation Education's website at www.uvm.edu/histpres/ncpe/chartgrad.html.

For architects practicing historic architecture, the minimum requirements are a degree in architecture or a state license to practice architecture plus one year of graduate study in either architectural preservation, American architectural history, preservation planning, or a closely related field or a least one year of full-time professional experience on historic preservation projects. Graduate study or professional experience should include detailed investigations of historic structures, preparation of historic structures research reports, and preparation of plans and specifications for preservation projects.

Salaries

Salary information for those working as restoration architects is limited, as they are typically grouped with building architects (see salary information for building architects earlier in this chapter).

In addition, salaries vary depending on what kind of firm or institution you work for. Jobs at museums, for example, may start in the mid $20,000s, while jobs with private architectural firms and working for the government can start in the mid $40,000s. Keep in mind, these are the starting salaries. If you are employed by an established firm that does high-quality work, you could command a substantially higher salary.

Landscape Architects

Everyone enjoys attractively designed residential areas, public parks, college campuses, shopping centers, golf courses, parkways, and industrial parks. Landscape architects design these areas so that they are not only functional but beautiful and compatible with the natural environment as well. They may plan the location of buildings, roads, and walkways and the arrangement of flowers, shrubs, and trees. They also may redesign streets to limit automobile traffic and to improve pedestrian access and safety. Natural resource conservation and historic preservation are other important objectives to which landscape architects may apply their knowledge of the environment as well as their design and artistic talents.

Landscape architects are hired by many types of organizations, from real estate development firms starting new projects to municipalities constructing airports or parks. They are often involved with the development of a site from its conception. Working with architects and engineers, they help determine the best arrangement of roads and buildings. Once these decisions are made, landscape architects create detailed plans indicating new topography, vegetation, walkways, and landscape amenities.

In planning a site, landscape architects first consider the nature and purpose of the project and the funds available. They analyze the natural elements of the site, such as the climate, soil, slope of the land, drainage, and vegetation. They observe where sunlight falls on the site at different times of the day and examine the site from various angles. They assess the effect of existing buildings, roads, walkways, and utilities on the project.

After studying and analyzing the site, they prepare a preliminary design. To account for the needs of the client as well as the conditions at the site, they may have to make many changes before a final design is approved. An increasing number of landscape architects use computer-aided design (CAD) systems to assist them in preparing their designs. Many landscape architects also use video simulation as a tool to help clients envision the landscape architects' ideas.

Throughout all phases of the design, landscape architects consult with other professionals involved in the project. Once the design is complete, they prepare a proposal for the client. They draw up detailed plans of the site, including written reports, sketches, models, photographs, land-use studies, and cost estimates, and submit them for approval by the client and by regulatory agencies. If the plans are approved, landscape architects prepare working drawings showing all existing and proposed features. They also outline in detail the methods of construction and draw up a list of necessary materials.

Landscape architects work on a wide variety of projects. Some specialize in a particular area, such as residential development, historic landscape restoration, waterfront improvement projects, parks and playgrounds, or shopping centers. Others work in regional planning and resource management; feasibility, environmental impact, and cost studies; or site construction. Some landscape architects teach at the college or university level. Although most landscape architects do at least some residential work, relatively few limit their practices to landscape design for individual homeowners because most residential landscape design projects are too small to provide suitable income compared with larger commercial or multiunit residential projects. Landscape architects who work for government agencies do similar work at national parks, government buildings, and other government-owned facilities. In addition, they may prepare environmental impact statements and studies on environmental issues such as public land-use planning.

In order to have a successful career in landscape architecture, you should appreciate nature, enjoy working with your hands, and possess strong analytical skills. Creative vision and artistic talent also are desirable qualities. Good oral communication skills are essential because landscape architects must be able to convey their ideas to other professionals and clients and to make presentations before large groups. Strong writing skills also are valuable, as is knowledge of computer applications of all kinds, including word processing, desktop publishing, and spreadsheets. Landscape architects use these tools to develop presentations, proposals, reports, and land impact studies for clients and colleagues in the field. People who are mechanically inclined or are curious about how things fit together and work would find landscape architecture a rewarding field.

Gardens are similar to buildings in that they require maintenance and upkeep, although gardens must be tended much more often and more rigorously than buildings. That's because gardens are dynamic; when a garden is mature or over-mature, replacements inevitably must be made for plants or trees that die. This keeps the garden looking presentable to the public.

Some landscape architects spend part of their time giving lectures to groups and garden clubs. You might also find that you're giving tours to some of the gardens you helped design. In cases like these, landscape architects double as garden historians, or someone with a background in history. If this interests you, you would combine history courses with horticulture courses. The job market for garden historians is fairly small, but it's growing as various conservation groups seek to reconstruct historic gardens. In order to create an authentic eighteenth-century garden as part of a historic home renovation, for example, a landscape architect who specializes in garden history would research and choose plants that were known and used in that time period. Much of the work involves looking at what was done historically in gardens, including the kinds of plants that were grown, how they were laid out, and the types of fencing that were used. In a few cases, even though a plant was appropriate to the period, it might not thrive in a particular location at the present time because of too much sunlight or too much shade. The landscape architect must then substitute another plant that would have been used but will grow better and flourish in that specific location under present-day conditions.

Job Outlook

According to government statistics, the outlook for the future of landscape architecture is good. In general, employment in this field will grow because the expertise of landscape architects will be highly sought after in the planning and development of new residential, commercial, and other types of construction. With land costs rising and the public desiring more beautiful spaces, the importance of good site planning and landscape design is growing. In addition, new demands to manage stormwater runoff in both existing and new landscapes, combined with the growing need to manage water resources, should cause increased demand for landscaper's services.

Landscape architects are playing more of a role in the protection of our environment and natural resources. More stringent environmental laws and regulations will push builders to seek the knowledge and services of landscape architects to help plan sites that meet these requirements. The goal of builders is increasingly to build structures that interact with the natural environment in the least disruptive way. More and more often, landscape architects are involved in preserving and restoring wetlands and other environmentally sensitive sites.

In addition to the work related to new development and construction, landscape architects are expected to be involved in historic preservation, land reclamation, and refurbishment of existing sites. They are also doing more residential design work as households spend more on landscaping than in the past. Because landscape architects can work on many different types of projects, they may have an easier time than other design professionals finding employment when traditional construction slows down, typically during periods of economic recession or during the colder months in some places.

New graduates can expect to face competition for jobs in the largest and most prestigious landscape architecture firms but should face good job opportunities overall as public demand for services increases. Opportunities will be best for landscape architects who develop strong technical skills—such as computer design—and communication skills, as well as knowledge of environmental codes and regulations. Those with additional training or experience in urban planning increase their opportunities for employment in landscape architecture firms that specialize in site planning as well as landscape design. Many employers prefer to hire entry-level landscape architects who have internship experience, which significantly reduces the amount of on-the-job training required.

Training and Education

Today's landscape architects not only have a naturally green thumb, but they have college educations as well. A bachelor's or master's degree is usually necessary for entry into the profession. Many bachelor's of landscape architecture (B.L.A.) programs take five years to complete; a master's degree can take two or three years. The two-year master's program is designed for bachelor's-level landscape architects; the three-year program is for students with bachelor's degrees in fields other than landscape architecture. Pursuing a master's degree helps refine your design abilities, focusing on more complex design problems. It also adds greatly to your employability and salary prospects. Those who pursue master's degrees usually have an area of focus or expertise, such as public space or historical landscaping. During your college experience, you can expect to take some of the following courses:

History of Landscape Architecture
Landscape Design and Construction
Landscape Ecology
Structural Design
Drafting
Urban and Regional Planning
Design and Color Theory
Soil Science
Geology
Meteorology
Topography
Plant Science (and other introductory horticulture courses)
Civil Engineering (covering grading, drainage, and pipe design)
Construction Law and Contracts
General Management

In addition to obtaining a degree in the field, almost all states require landscape architects to be licensed. Licensing is based on passing the Landscape Architect Registration Examination (LARE), sponsored by the Council of Landscape Architecture Registration Boards (www.clarb.org). Admission to the exam usually requires a college degree and one to four years of work experience. Some states require an additional exam focusing on the laws or plant materials indigenous to that state. Landscape architects employed by the federal government are not required to be licensed.

Before licensing, a new hire typically is called a landscape architect intern. The title is misleading because interns can, depending upon their employer's requirements, perform all the duties of a licensed landscape architect. However, the intern works under the guidance of a licensed practitioner until he or she has passed the exam.

Salaries

According to government statistics, the median annual earnings for landscape architects are about $53,100. The middle 50 percent of all those working in the United States earn between $40,900 and $70,400. The lowest 10 percent earn less than $32,400, and the highest 10 percent earn over $90,900. Architectural, engineering, and related services employed more landscape architects than any other group of industries, and there the median annual earnings are about $51,700, slightly less than for all jobs combined.

Those working for the federal government earn a higher wage than those in private industry. In 2005, the average annual salary for all landscape architects working for the government in non-supervisory, supervisory, and managerial positions was $74,500. Keep in mind that those working for state and local governments may earn less, depending on location.

Benefits, such as vacation time, health care, and retirement funds, vary depending on the type of organization. Because many landscape architects work for small firms or are self-employed, benefits tend to be less generous than those provided to workers in large organizations. Also, working for the government—local, state, or federal—provides substantial benefits in addition to salary.

A Lasting Impact

Architects of all kinds and persuasions help shape, grow, and preserve the world around us. If you think you might like to make a lasting impact on the buildings we use and the gardens we walk through and enjoy, then you should consider an architectural career. This is creative and meticulous work that truly makes a difference.

CHAPTER FIVE

Surveyors and Mapmakers

A carefully thought-out and well-designed map is a powerful tool. Maps provide a wealth of information in one concise, visual representation. Because we live in a highly visual society, an increasing number of individuals and firms are using maps to analyze and illustrate spatial problems. Maps, from the very simple to the extremely complex, can be generated from detailed site visits and from models and graphics based on air photos and existing maps. They are created using all types of formats, including Internet websites, animated presentations, CD-ROM, and traditional paper versions. Modern mapmakers create custom maps and graphics for a variety of purposes, including the following:

- courtroom analysis, display, and presentation
- environmental problem solving
- universities, stadiums, and other sports facilities
- fairgrounds, festivals, and race tracks
- transportation and parking planning (evacuation, shuttle, and recycling routes)
- sales and marketing presentations and reports
- museum displays
- providing directions

The purpose of a map is to illustrate and convey information. To that end, it must be precise and accurate. A great deal of time, research, calculation, and input from a variety of key sources goes into creating a useful map, making this area a good one for those who are perfectionists at heart.

Land Surveyors

Surveying is the process of accurately determining the space between points and the distances and angles between them. These points are usually associated with positions on the surface of the earth, such as points from one riverbank to the opposite side, and are often used to establish land maps and boundaries for ownership or governmental purposes. During the course of their work, surveyors use elements of geometry, engineering, math, physics, and law.

Surveying is necessary to the planning and execution of nearly every form of construction—from determining the boundaries between plots of land to constructing a skyscraper in the middle of a large city. Today, surveying is mainly used in the fields of transportation, building and construction, communications, mapping, and defining legal boundaries for land ownership. Because these fields exist in communities both large and small, there are always jobs for surveyors, no matter where you live.

So what exactly do land surveyors do? Land surveyors provide the calculations and measurements that form the foundation for creating a map of a geographic area. They establish official land, air space, and water boundaries; write descriptions of land for deeds, leases, and other legal documents; define air space for airports; and measure construction and mineral sites. Survey technicians, who operate surveying instruments and collect information, assist them in their work.

Land surveyors manage one or more survey parties that measure distances, directions, and angles between points and elevations of points, lines, and contours on the earth's surface. They plan the fieldwork, select known survey reference points, and determine the precise location of all important features of the survey area. They research legal records and look for evidence of previous boundaries. They record the results of the survey, verify the accuracy of data, and prepare plans, maps, and reports.

A survey party gathers the information needed by the land surveyor. A typical survey party is made up of a party chief and several survey technicians and helpers. The party chief, who may be either a land surveyor or a senior survey technician, leads all of the day-to-day work activities. Survey technicians adjust and operate surveying instruments and electronic distance-measuring equipment.

Survey technicians position and hold the vertical rods or targets that the theodolite operator sights on to measure angles, distances, or elevations. (Theodolites are instruments on tripods used to take measurements.) These assistants may also hold measuring tapes and chains if electronic distance-measuring equipment is not used. Survey technicians compile notes, make sketches, and enter the data obtained from various instruments into computers. Some survey parties include laborers or helpers to clear brush from sight lines, drive stakes, carry equipment, and perform other, less-skilled duties.

New technology is changing the nature of the work of surveyors and survey technicians. For larger projects, surveyors are increasingly using the Global Positioning System (GPS), a satellite system that precisely locates points on the earth using radio signals transmitted by satellites. To use it, a surveyor places a satellite receiver about the size of a backpack on a desired point. The receiver collects information from several differently positioned satellites at once to locate its precise position. Two receivers are generally operated simultaneously, one at a known point and the other at the unknown point. The receiver can also be placed in a vehicle to trace out road systems or for other uses. As the cost of the receivers falls, much more surveying work will be done by GPS.

Work Settings and Hours

Surveyors work regular hours each week. They usually work an eight-hour day, five days a week, and spend a lot of time outdoors. Sometimes they work longer hours during the summer, when weather and light conditions are most suitable for fieldwork. Occasionally, they may commute long distances, stay overnight, or even temporarily relocate near a survey site.

Land surveyors and technicians do active and sometimes strenuous work. They often stand for long periods, walk long distances, and climb hills with heavy packs of instruments and equipment. They are also exposed to all types of weather. While all the fresh air might sound pleasant—and mostly it is—there are times when surveyors have to work in less than ideal conditions, like rain and snow. Surveyors also spend considerable time in offices planning surveys, analyzing data, and preparing reports and maps. Most computations and map drafting are done at a computer. Indeed, those working solely as mapping scientists spend almost all their time in offices.

Surveyors are employed by only a few different kinds of companies or organizations. Engineering, architectural, and surveying firms employ nearly three-fifths of all surveyors, while federal, state, and local government agencies employ an additional one-fourth. Most surveyors in state and local government work for highway departments and urban planning and redevelopment agencies. Major federal government employers are the U.S. Geological Survey (www.usgs.gov), the Bureau of Land Management (www.blm.gov), the Army Corps of Engineers (www.usace.army.mil), the U.S. Forest Service (www.fs.fed.us), and the National Oceanic and Atmospheric Administration (www.noaa.gov). Construction firms, mining and oil and gas extraction companies, and public utilities also employ surveyors.

Training and Education

Most states have licensure requirements for surveyors; in particular, those who establish official boundaries must be licensed by the state in which they work. Most people prepare to be a licensed surveyor by combining postsecondary school courses in surveying with extensive on-the-job training. More than two dozen universities offer four-year programs leading to a B.S. degree in surveying. Junior and community colleges, technical institutes, and vocational schools offer one-, two-, and three-year programs in both surveying and surveying technology.

For licensure, most state licensing boards require that individuals pass two written examinations, one prepared by the state and one given by the National Council of Examiners for Engineering and Surveying (www.ncees.org). In addition, they must meet varying standards of formal education and work experience in the field. In the past, many surveyors started as members of survey crews and worked their way up to licensed surveyor with little formal training in surveying. However, due to advancing technology and an increase in licensing standards, more formal education is now required. Most states require some formal post–high school education courses and five to twelve years of surveying experience to gain licensure. However, requirements vary among the states. Generally, the quickest route is a combination of four years of college, two to four years of experience (a few states do not require any), and passing the licensing examinations. An increasing number of states require a bachelor's degree in surveying or in a closely related field, such as civil engineering or forestry, with courses in surveying.

High school students interested in surveying should take courses in algebra, geometry, trigonometry, drafting, mechanical drawing, and computer science. High school graduates with no formal training in surveying usually start as helpers. Beginners with postsecondary school training in surveying can generally start as technicians. With on-the-job experience and formal training in surveying either in an institutional program or from a correspondence school, workers may advance to senior survey technician, then to party chief, and finally, in some cases, to licensed surveyor (depending on state licensing requirements).

A voluntary certification program for survey technicians is available from the American Congress on Surveying and Mapping (www.acsm.net). Technicians are certified at four levels requiring progressive amounts of experience; technicians who qualify are certified at a higher level after passing a written examination. Although not required for state licensure, many employers require certification for promotion to more responsible positions.

So, how do you know if you have what it takes to succeed in this job? Surveyors should have the ability to visualize objects, distances, sizes, and other abstract forms and to work precisely and accurately because mistakes can be very costly. Surveying is a cooperative process, so good interpersonal skills and the ability to work as part of a team are important. Leadership qualities are important for party chief and other supervisory positions. Members of a survey party must be in good physical condition to work outdoors and carry equipment over difficult terrain. They also need good eyesight, coordination, and hearing to communicate by hand or voice signals. If you possess many or all of these skills, then a career in surveying might be right for you.

Salaries

According to government statistics, the median annual earnings of surveyors are about $43,000. The middle 50 percent of those working earn between $32,000 and $57,200. The lowest 10 percent earn less than $24,600, and the highest 10 percent earn more than $71,600. The median earnings of surveyors employed in architectural, engineering, and related services are $41,700.

Technicians, who have less formal training, earn less. Their median annual earnings are about $30,400. The middle 50 percent earn between $23,600 and $40,100. The lowest 10 percent earn less than $19,100, and the highest 10 percent earn more than $51,100. The median annual earnings of surveying and mapping technicians specifically employed in architectural, engineering, and related services are $28,600, while those employed by local governments have higher median annual earnings of about $34,800.

Mapmakers

There are a wide variety of types of maps made by mapmakers. For example, the map you're most used to seeing in a classroom is a topographical map. A topographical map is a graphic representation of a portion of the earth's surface drawn to scale, as seen from above. It uses colors, symbols, and labels to represent features found on the ground. A map provides information on the location of and the distance between ground features, such as populated places and routes of travel and communication. It also indicates variations in terrain, heights of natural features, and the extent of vegetation cover. Another type of map is the historical map. Historical maps illustrate what a place or environment looked like at one point in time. It may be a layout of a town or the coverage of glaciers from thousands of years ago.

Mapmakers collect geographic information and prepare maps and charts of large areas. Like land surveyors, they measure, map, and chart the earth's surface but generally cover much larger areas. However, mapping scientists work mainly in offices and seldom, if ever, visit the sites they are mapping. Mapmakers include workers in several related, but different, occupations:

- **Cartographers** prepare maps in either digital or graphic form using information provided by geodetic surveys, aerial photographs, and satellite data.
- **Photogrammetrists** prepare maps and drawings by measuring and interpreting aerial photographs, using analytical processes and mathematical formulas. They make detailed maps of areas that are inaccessible or difficult to survey by other methods.
- **Map editors** develop and verify map contents from aerial photographs and other reference sources.

Some surveyors perform specialized functions that are closer to mapping science than traditional surveying. For example, geodetic surveyors use high-accuracy techniques, including satellite observations, to measure large areas of the earth's surface. Geophysical prospecting surveyors mark sites for subsurface exploration, usually petroleum related. Finally, marine surveyors survey harbors, rivers, and other bodies of water to determine shorelines, topography of the bottom, water depth, and other features.

The work of mapping scientists is changing due to new technologies. The technologies include the Global Positioning System (GPS); Geographic Information Systems (GIS), which are computerized data banks of spatial data; new earth resources data satellites; and improved aerial photography. From the older specialties of photogrammetrist or cartographer, a new type of mapping scientist is emerging. The geographic information specialist combines the functions of mapping science and surveying into a broader field concerned with the collection and analysis of geographic spatial information.

Cartographers

Cartography is the art and science of expressing the known physical features of the earth graphically with maps and charts. Cartographers measure, map, and chart the earth's surface. Their work involves everything from performing geographical research and compiling data to actually producing maps. Cartographers collect, analyze, and interpret both spatial data—such as latitude, longitude, elevation, and distance—and nonspatial data—for example, population density, land-use patterns, annual precipitation levels, and demographic characteristics. Their maps may give both physical and social characteristics of the land.

Training and Education

Cartographers and photogrammetrists usually have bachelor's degrees in engineering or a physical science, although it is possible to enter these jobs through experience as a photogrammetric or cartographic technician. Most cartographic and photogrammetry technicians have had some specialized postsecondary school training. Some states even require photogrammetrists to be licensed as surveyors.

Computers are key to landing a job and advancing in the field. With the development of GIS, cartographers, photogrammetrists, and other mapping scientists now need more education and experience in the use of computers than in the past. The American Society for Photogrammetry and Remote Sensing (www.asprs .org) offers voluntary certification programs for photogrammetrists and mapping scientists. To qualify for these professional distinctions, individuals must meet work experience standards and pass an oral or written examination.

Salaries

According to government statistics, the median annual earnings of cartographers and photogrammetrists are about $46,000. The middle 50 percent of those working in the field earn between $35,200 and $59,800. The lowest 10 percent earn less than $28,200, and the highest 10 percent earn more than $74,400.

Job Outlook

According to government statistics, the overall employment of surveyors, cartographers, photogrammetrists, and surveying technicians is expected to grow about as fast as the average for all occupations through the year 2014. The widespread availability and use of advanced technologies, such as the global positioning system or GPS and remote sensing, will continue to increase both the accuracy and productivity of those working in the field, which will limit the availability of jobs to some extent.

Opportunities for surveyors, cartographers, and photogrammetrists should remain concentrated in architectural, engineering, and related services firms. Areas such as urban planning, emergency preparedness, and natural resource exploration and mapping also should provide employment growth, particularly with regard to producing maps for the management of emergencies and updating maps with the newly available technology. However, employment may fluctuate from year to year with changies in construction activity or in the need for mapping to support land and resource management.

Opportunities should be stronger for professional surveyors than for surveying and mapping technicians. Advancements in technology, such as total stations and GPS, have made surveying parties smaller than they were in the past. As a result of the trend toward more complex technology, upgraded licensing requirements, and the increased demand for geographic spatial data (as opposed to traditional surveying services), there will be greater opportunities for surveyors and mapping scientists who have at least a bachelor's degree. Opportunities for technicians should be available in basic data-entry work. However, many people possess the basic skills needed to qualify for these jobs, so applicants for technician jobs may face competition.

Growth in construction should create jobs for surveyors who lay out streets, shopping centers, housing developments, factories, office buildings, and recreation areas. Road and highway construction and improvement also should generate new surveying positions. However, employment may fluctuate from year to year along with construction activity. Overall, however, if you're lucky enough to land any one of these jobs, you'll find there's a lot of stability in the position and autonomy in the work.

Mapping the Future

Surveying and mapmaking are two very different careers, although one often depends on the other. If you find yourself more attracted to steady, reliable work, where the tasks of the job are the same, then surveying might be a good fit for you. If you're a more creative person and you enjoy the process of puzzling out problems, then mapmaking or cartography might be a better option. Regardless of which area you choose, you'll be sure to find one of these jobs satisfies the perfectionist in you.

CHAPTER SIX

Engineers

H ave you always enjoyed building things? As a child, did you construct elaborate buildings and structures out of boxes or Legos? Have you ever taken apart a mechanical object, such as a clock or radio, just to see how it looked inside? If you have an insatiable curiosity about how things work, then you just might find engineering to be the perfect career for you.

Engineers are those who create careers out of exploring how things work and designing machines, structures, and products. They apply the theories and principles of science and math to the economical solution of practical technical problems. Often their work is the link between a scientific discovery and its application. Engineers perform exacting tasks as they design machinery, products, systems, and processes for efficient and economical performance. They design industrial machinery and equipment for manufacturing goods and defense and weapons systems for the armed forces. Many engineers design, plan, and supervise the construction of buildings, highways, and rapid-transit systems, working with architects and surveyors. They also design and develop consumer products and systems for control and automation of manufacturing, business, and management processes. Complex projects require many engineers, each working with a small part of the job. Supervisory engineers are responsible for major components or entire projects.

Engineers consider many factors in developing a new product. For example, in developing an industrial robot, they determine precisely what function it needs to perform, design and test components, fit them together in an integrated plan, and evaluate the design's overall effectiveness, cost, reliability, and safety. This process applies to products as varied as computers, gas turbines, generators, helicopters, and toys.

There are several types of engineers. In addition to design and development, engineers work in testing, production, and maintenance. They supervise production in factories, determine causes of breakdowns, and test manufactured products to maintain quality. They also estimate the time and cost to complete projects.

Engineering is a high-tech field that's increasingly dependent on the work of computers. Engineers use computers to simulate and test how a machine, structure, or system operates. Many also use computer-aided design systems to produce and analyze designs. There are even engineers designing the computers the engineers use to do their work.

Engineering Specializations

Most engineers specialize in one particular kind of engineering, and there are more than twenty-five major specialties recognized by professional societies. Within the major branches are numerous subdivisions. For example, structural and transportation engineering, as well as environmental engineering—a small but growing discipline involved with identifying, solving, and alleviating environmental problems—are subdivisions of civil engineering. Engineers also may specialize in one industry, such as motor vehicles, or in one field of technology, such as propulsion or guidance systems. The following are brief descriptions of just a few of the engineering specializations:

- **Aerospace engineers** design, develop, and test aircraft, spacecraft, and missiles and supervise the manufacture of these products. Those who work with aircraft are called aeronautical engineers, and those working specifically with spacecraft are astronautical engineers. Aerospace engineers develop new technologies for use in aviation, defense systems, and space exploration, often specializing in areas such as structural design, guidance, navigation and control, instrumentation and communication, or production methods. They also may specialize in a particular type of aerospace product, such as commercial aircraft, military fighter jets, helicopters, spacecraft, or missiles and rockets, and may become experts in aerodynamics, thermodynamics, celestial mechanics, propulsion, acoustics, or guidance and control systems.

- **Agricultural engineers** apply engineering technology and science to agriculture and the efficient use of biological resources. They design agricultural machinery and equipment and agricultural structures. Some specialize in areas such as power systems and machinery design, structures and environmental engineering, and food and bioprocess engineering. They develop ways to conserve soil and water and to improve the processing of agricultural products.
- **Biomedical engineers** develop devices and procedures that solve medical and health-related problems by combining their knowledge of biology and medicine with engineering principles and practices. Many do research, along with life scientists, chemists, and medical scientists, to develop and evaluate systems and products such as artificial organs, prostheses (artificial devices that replace missing body parts), instrumentation, medical information systems, and health management and care delivery systems. Biomedical engineers may also design devices used in various medical procedures, imaging systems such as magnetic resonance imaging (MRI), and devices for automating insulin injections or controlling body functions. Most engineers in this specialty need a sound background in another engineering specialty, such as mechanical or electronics engineering, in addition to specialized biomedical training. Some specialties

within biomedical engineering include biomaterials, bio-
mechanics, medical imaging, rehabilitation engineering, and
orthopedic engineering.

- **Chemical engineers** apply the principles of chemistry to
  solve problems involving the production or use of chemicals
  and biochemicals. They design equipment and processes for
  large-scale chemical manufacturing, plan and test methods
  of manufacturing products and treating by-products, and
  supervise production. Chemical engineers work in a variety
  of manufacturing industries other than chemical manufacturing, such as those producing energy, electronics, food,
  clothing, and paper. They also work in health care, biotech-
  nology, and business services. Some may specialize in a
  particular chemical process, such as oxidation or poly-
  merization. Others specialize in a particular field, such
  as materials science, or in the development of specific
  products.

- **Civil engineers** design and supervise the construction of
  roads, buildings, airports, tunnels, dams, bridges, and water
  supply and sewage systems. They must consider many
  factors in the design process, from the construction costs
  and expected lifetime of a project to government regulations and potential environmental hazards, such as earth-
  quakes. Civil engineering, considered one of the oldest
  engineering disciplines, encompasses many specialties. The
  major specialties are structural, water resources, construction, environmental, transportation, and geotechnical
  engineering. Others may work in design, construction,
  research, and teaching.

- **Computer hardware engineers** research, design, develop,
  test, and oversee the installation of computer hardware and
  supervise its manufacture and installation. Hardware refers
  to computer chips, circuit boards, computer systems, and
  related equipment such as keyboards, modems, and printers. The work of computer hardware engineers is very

similar to that of electronics engineers, but, unlike electronics engineers, computer hardware engineers work exclusively with computers and computer-related equipment. The rapid advances in computer technology are largely a result of the research, development, and design efforts of computer hardware engineers.

- **Electrical engineers** design, develop, test, and supervise the manufacture of electrical equipment. Some of this equipment includes electric motors; machinery controls, lighting, and wiring in buildings; automobiles; aircraft; radar and navigation systems; and power-generating, -controlling, and transmission devices used by electric utilities. Although the terms *electrical engineering* and *electronics engineering* often are used interchangeably in academia and industry, electrical engineers have traditionally focused on the generation and supply of power, whereas electronics engineers have worked on applications of electricity to control systems or signal processing. Electrical engineers specialize in areas such as power systems engineering or electrical equipment manufacturing.
- **Electronics engineers** are responsible for a wide range of technologies, from portable music players to the Global Positioning System (GPS), which can continuously pinpoint the location of a vehicle. Electronics engineers design, develop, test, and supervise the manufacture of electronic equipment, such as broadcast and communications systems. Many electronics engineers also work in areas closely related to computers. Electronics engineers specialize in areas such as communications, signal processing, and control systems or have a specialty within one of these areas—industrial robot control systems or aviation electronics, for example.
- **Environmental engineers** develop solutions to environmental problems using the principles of biology and chemistry. They are involved in water and air pollution control, recycling, waste disposal, and public health issues.

Environmental engineers conduct hazardous-waste management studies in which they evaluate the significance of the hazard, advise on treatment and containment, and develop regulations to prevent mishaps. They design municipal water supply and industrial wastewater treatment systems. They conduct research on the environmental impact of proposed construction projects, analyze scientific data, and perform quality-control checks. Environmental engineers are concerned with local and worldwide environmental issues. They study and attempt to minimize the effects of acid rain, global warming, automobile emissions, and ozone depletion. They may also be involved in the protection of wildlife. Many environmental engineers work as consultants, helping their clients to comply with regulations and to clean up hazardous sites.

- **Health and safety engineers,** except mining safety engineers and inspectors, promote workplace or product safety by applying knowledge of industrial processes and mechanical, chemical, and human performance principles. Using this specialized knowledge, they identify and measure potential hazards to people or property, such as the risk of fires or the dangers involved in handling toxic chemicals. Health and safety engineers develop procedures and designs to reduce the risk of injury or damage. Some work in manufacturing industries to ensure that the designs of new products do not create unnecessary hazards. They must be able to anticipate, recognize, and evaluate hazardous conditions, as well as develop hazard-control methods.

- **Industrial engineers** determine the most effective ways to use the basic factors of production—people, machines, materials, information, and energy—to make a product or to provide a service. They are mostly concerned with increasing productivity through the management of people, methods of business organization, and technology. To solve organizational, production, and related problems efficiently,

industrial engineers carefully study the product requirements, use mathematical methods to meet those requirements, and design manufacturing and information systems.
They develop management control systems to aid in financial planning and cost analysis and design production planning and control systems to coordinate activities and ensure
product quality. They also design or improve systems for
the physical distribution of goods and services, as well as
determine the most efficient plant locations. Industrial
engineers develop wage and salary administration systems
and job evaluation programs.

- **Marine engineers and naval architects** are involved in the
design, construction, and maintenance of ships, boats, and
related equipment. They design and supervise the construction of everything from aircraft carriers to submarines,
from sailboats to tankers. Naval architects work on the basic
design of ships, including hull form and stability. Marine
engineers work on the propulsion, steering, and other systems of ships. Marine engineers and naval architects apply
knowledge from a range of fields to the entire design and
production process of all water vehicles. Workers who
operate or supervise the operation of marine machinery on
ships and other vessels also may be called marine engineers
or, more frequently, ship engineers.

- **Materials engineers** are involved in the development,
processing, and testing of the materials used to create a
range of products, from computer chips and television
screens to golf clubs and snow skis. They work with metals,
ceramics, plastics, semiconductors, and composites to create
new materials that meet certain mechanical, electrical, and
chemical requirements. They also are involved in selecting
materials for new applications. Materials engineers have
developed the ability to create and then study materials at
an atomic level, using advanced processes to replicate the
characteristics of materials and their components with

computers. Most materials engineers specialize in a particular material. For example, metallurgical engineers specialize in metals such as steel, and ceramic engineers develop ceramic materials and the processes for making ceramic materials into useful products such as glassware or fiber optic communication lines.

- **Mechanical engineers** research, develop, design, manufacture, and test tools, engines, machines, and other mechanical devices. They work on power-producing machines such as electric generators, internal combustion engines, and steam and gas turbines, as well as power-using machines such as refrigeration and air-conditioning equipment, machine tools, material handling systems, elevators and escalators, industrial production equipment, and robots used in manufacturing. Mechanical engineers also design tools that other engineers need for their work. Mechanical engineering is one of the broadest engineering disciplines, and many work in production operations in manufacturing or in agriculture, maintenance, or technical sales.

- **Mining and geological engineers**, including mining safety engineers, find, extract, and prepare coal, metals, and minerals for use by manufacturing industries and utilities. They design open-pit and underground mines, supervise the construction of mine shafts and tunnels in underground operations, and devise methods for transporting minerals to processing plants. Mining engineers are responsible for the safe, economical, and environmentally sound operation of mines. Some mining engineers work with geologists and metallurgical engineers to locate and appraise new ore deposits. Others develop new mining equipment or direct mineral-processing operations that separate minerals from the dirt, rock, and other materials with which they are mixed. Mining engineers frequently specialize in the mining of one mineral or metal, such as coal or gold. With increased emphasis on protecting the environment, many mining engineers work to solve problems related to land reclamation and water and air pollution. Mining safety engineers use their knowledge of mine design and practices to ensure the safety of workers and to comply with state and federal safety regulations. They inspect walls and roof surfaces, monitor air quality, and examine mining equipment for compliance with safety practices.

- **Nuclear engineers** research and develop the processes, instruments, and systems used to derive benefits from nuclear energy and radiation. They design, develop, monitor, and operate nuclear plants to generate power. They may work on the nuclear fuel cycle—the production, handling, and use of nuclear fuel and the safe disposal of waste produced by the generation of nuclear energy—or on the development of fusion energy. Some specialize in the development of nuclear power sources for spacecraft; others find industrial and medical uses for radioactive materials, as in equipment used to diagnose and treat medical problems.

- **Petroleum engineers** search the world for reservoirs containing oil or natural gas. Once these resources are discovered, petroleum engineers work with geologists and other specialists to understand the geologic formation and properties of the rock containing the reservoir, determine the drilling methods to be used, and monitor drilling and production operations. They design equipment and processes to achieve the maximum profitable recovery of oil and gas. Because only a small proportion of oil and gas in a reservoir flows out under natural forces, petroleum engineers develop and use various enhanced recovery methods. These include injecting water, chemicals, gases, or steam into an oil reservoir to force out more of the oil and doing computer-controlled drilling or fracturing to connect a larger area of a reservoir to a single well. Because even the best techniques in use today recover only a portion of the oil and gas in a reservoir, petroleum engineers research and develop technology and methods to increase recovery and lower the cost of drilling and production operations.

Engineers in each branch have knowledge and training that can be applied to many fields. Electrical and electronics engineers, for example, work in the medical, computer, missile guidance, and power distribution fields. Because there are many separate problems to solve in a large engineering project, engineers in one field often work closely with other engineers and specialists in scientific and business occupations.

In addition to working directly in the field of engineering, some with training as an engineer work in other areas, such as management or sales. In these jobs, an engineering background enables workers to discuss the technical aspects of a product and assist in planning its installation or use. Sales positions are particularly good for those who like to teach and interact with others. If you're a people person, you should consider this aspect of engineering.

Work Settings and Hours

Engineers of all sorts work in a variety of settings. Many engineers work in laboratories, industrial plants, or construction sites, where they inspect, supervise, or solve on-site problems. Others work in an office almost all of the time. Engineers in branches such as civil engineering may even work outdoors part of the time. A few engineers travel extensively to plants or other construction sites to inspect the work.

Most engineers put in a lot of time at work; typically, they have a fifty-hour workweek. Because engineers must stay current with rapidly changing technology, they may have to attend conferences or take classes at colleges and universities in their spare time. This makes for a full week, although many cite job satisfaction and earnings as making this time spent worthwhile.

Deadlines or design standards may bring extra pressure to a job. When this happens, engineers may experience considerable stress. The stress that comes with this type of job is one of the few downsides of the profession. How well you handle stress and whether or not you thrive on it is something to consider.

Sometimes the work can be very hands on. Many engineers actually build the machines they design. These engineers enjoy getting dirty, lying on the floor under the electrical enclosure, pulling wire and cable, and using their own two hands to create something new.

Engineering can be either very autonomous or very collaborative. This, of course, depends on the nature of the work and whether or not the work hours are tied to a production schedule. Some engineers focus on one piece of a product, so they must work harmoniously with those producing the other parts. Others engineer whole products or structures.

Job Outlook

According to government statistics provided by the U.S. Department of Labor, engineers hold an astounding 1.4 million jobs in the United States. About 555,000 of these are found in manufacturing industries; another 378,000 wage and salary jobs are in the professional, scientific, and technical services sector, primarily in architectural, engineering, and related services and in scientific research and development services. Many engineers also work in the construction, transportation, telecommunications, and utilities industries. Federal, state, and local governments employed about 194,000 engineers in 2004. About 91,000 of these were in the federal government, mainly in the U.S. Departments of Defense, Transportation, Agriculture, Interior, and Energy and in the National Aeronautics and Space Administration. Most engineers in state and local government agencies work in highway and public works departments. In 2004, about 41,000 engineers were self-employed, many as consultants.

No matter where you live, you can find work as an engineer. That's because engineers are employed in every state, in small and large cities, and in rural areas. Some branches of engineering are concentrated in particular industries and geographic areas—for example, petroleum engineering jobs tend to be located in areas with sizable petroleum deposits, such as Texas, Louisiana, Oklahoma, Alaska, and California. Others, such as civil engineering jobs, are widely dispersed, and engineers in these fields often move from place to place to work on different projects.

Engineers have traditionally been concentrated in manufacturing industries, in which they will continue to be needed to design, build, test, and improve manufactured products. However, increasing employment of engineers in faster-growing service industries should generate most of the employment growth. Overall job opportunities in engineering are expected to be good for the foreseeable future.

Competitive pressures and advancing technology will force companies to improve and update product designs. This is where engineers come in. Employers will rely on engineers to increase productivity in order to increase their production of goods and services. New technologies continue to improve the design process, enabling engineers to produce and analyze various product designs much more rapidly than in the past.

There are many well-trained, often English-speaking engineers available around the world willing to work at much lower salaries than are U.S. engineers. The rise of the Internet has made it relatively easy for much of the engineering work previously done by engineers in this country to be done by engineers in other countries, a factor that will tend to hold down employment growth. Even so, the need for onsite engineers to interact with other employees and with clients will remain.

Many engineers work on long-term research and development projects or in other activities that continue even during economic slowdowns. In industries such as electronics and aerospace, however, large cutbacks in defense expenditures and in government funding for research and development have resulted in significant layoffs of engineers in the past. The trend toward contracting for engineering work with engineering services firms, both domestic and foreign, has had the same result.

It is important for engineers at all levels to continue their education throughout their careers because much of their value to employers depends on their knowledge of the latest technology. Engineers in high-technology areas, such as advanced electronics or information technology, may find that technical knowledge can become outdated rapidly. By keeping current in their fields, engineers are able to deliver the best solutions and greatest value to their employers. Engineers who have not kept current in the field may find themselves passed over for promotions or vulnerable to layoffs.

Training and Education

Working as an engineer requires a good deal of formal education. A bachelor's degree in engineering from an accredited engineering program is usually required for most beginning engineering jobs. College graduates with degrees in a physical science or mathematics may occasionally qualify for some engineering jobs, particularly in specialties in high demand. Most engineering degrees are granted in branches such as electrical, mechanical, or civil engineering. However, those trained in one branch may work in another. This flexibility allows employers to meet staffing needs in new technologies and specialties in short supply. It also allows engineers to shift to fields that match their interests more closely or that have better employment prospects.

In addition to the standard engineering degree, many colleges offer degrees in engineering technology, which are offered as either two- or four-year programs. These programs prepare students for practical design and production work rather than for jobs that require more theoretical, scientific, and mathematical knowledge. Graduates of four-year technology programs may get jobs similar to those obtained by graduates with bachelor's degrees in engineering. In fact, some employers regard them as having skills between those of a technician and an engineer.

Graduate training is essential for engineering faculty positions but is not required for the majority of entry-level jobs. Many engineers obtain master's degrees to learn new technology, to broaden their education, and to enhance promotion opportunities. If you ever want to teach engineering at a college or university, you'll need at least a master's and often a doctorate in order to do so.

You'll be happy with the number of choices of schools available to you in this area. Approximately 350 colleges and universities offer a bachelor's degree in engineering, and nearly 300 colleges offer a bachelor's degree in engineering technology, although not all are accredited programs. Although most institutions offer programs in the larger branches of engineering, only a few offer some of the smaller specialties. Also, programs of the same title may vary in content, so be sure to ask lots of questions about the program before you commit to it. For example, some emphasize industrial practices, preparing students for a job in industry, while others are more theoretical and are better for students preparing for graduate work. Admissions requirements for undergraduate engineering schools include courses in advanced high school mathematics and the physical sciences.

Bachelor's degree programs in engineering are typically designed to last four years, but many students find that it takes between four and five years to complete their studies. In a typical four-year college curriculum, the first two years are spent studying basic sciences (mathematics, physics, and chemistry), introductory engineering, humanities, social sciences, and English.

In the last two years of the program, most courses are in engineering, usually with a concentration in one branch. For example, the last two years of an aerospace program might include courses such as fluid mechanics, heat transfer, applied aerodynamics, analytical mechanics, flight vehicle design, trajectory dynamics, and aerospace propulsion systems. Some programs offer a general engineering curriculum; students then specialize in graduate school or on the job.

A few engineering schools and two-year colleges have agreements whereby the two-year college provides the initial engineering education and the engineering school automatically admits students for their last two years. In addition, a few engineering schools have arrangements whereby a student spends three years in a liberal arts college studying pre-engineering subjects and two years in the engineering school and receives a bachelor's degree from each. Some colleges and universities offer five-year master's degree programs. Some five- or even six-year cooperative plans combine classroom study and practical work, permitting students to gain valuable experience and finance part of their education.

Any engineer interested in becoming a machine designer or automation engineer should seriously consider the multidisciplinary approach of taking courses in both mechanical and electrical engineering. Machine design requires a broad knowledge base; one must understand mechanics in order to design efficient control systems, and one must understand control systems in order to design machines that can be effectively controlled. The best machine designers have dual degrees in these fields.

Registration

All fifty states and the District of Columbia require registration for engineers whose work may affect life, health, or property, or who offer their services to the public. Registration generally requires a degree from an engineering program accredited by the Accreditation Board for Engineering and Technology (www.abet .org), four years of relevant work experience, and passing a state examination. Some states will not register people with degrees in engineering technology.

Necessary Skills

There are a variety of skills you should possess in order to succeed in this field. As an engineer, you should be able to work as part of a team, should be creative, and should have an analytical mind and capacity for detail. In addition, you should be able to express yourself well both orally and in writing.

Engineering is a job that entails some writing, research, diplomacy, and group management. Getting people to participate and work together as a team is only half of the "diplomat" part of the job: keeping them interested in a project is far more challenging. Balancing the personalities in the group is essential, and often the key to getting the information you need and getting it down right the first time is to learn quickly who can work together and who can't; then you should decide how to get input from those who don't work well together so that none are shut out from participating. Sometimes the fastest way to complete a project is not in a group, but working one-on-one with several people and coordinating and sharing the information as it comes in.

Advancement

Beginning engineering graduates usually do routine work under the supervision of experienced engineers and, in larger companies, may also receive formal classroom or seminar-type training. As they gain knowledge and experience, they are assigned more difficult tasks with greater independence to develop designs, solve problems, and make decisions. Eventually, beginning engineers work with some degree of autonomy.

Supervision and management positions are generally the highest positions to which you could advance. Engineers may supervise a staff or team of engineers and technicians. Some eventually become engineering managers or enter other managerial, management support, or sales jobs. You might considering obtaining a graduate degree in engineering or business administration to improve your advancement opportunities.

Salaries

Earnings for engineers vary significantly by specialty, industry, and education. Even so, as a group, engineers earn some of the highest average starting salaries among those holding bachelor's degrees. Table 1 shows average starting salary offers for engineers by specialty.

TABLE 1. Average Starting Salaries by Degree and Engineering Specialty

CURRICULUM	BACHELOR'S	MASTER'S	PH.D.
Aerospace/aeronautical/ astronautical	$50,993	$62,930	$72,529
Agricultural	$46,172	$53,022	
Bioengineering/ biomedical	$48,503	$59,667	
Chemical	$53,813	$57,260	$79,591
Civil	$43,679	$48,050	$59,625
Computer	$52,464	$60,354	$69,625
Electrical/electronics	$51,888	$64,416	$80,206
Environmental/ environmental health	$47,384		
Industrial/manufacturing	$49,567	$56,561	$85,000
Materials	$50,982		
Mechanical	$50,236	$59,880	$68,299
Mining/mineral	$48,643		
Nuclear	$51,182	$58,814	
Petroleum	$61,516	$58,000	

Source: 2005 National Association of Colleges and Employers survey

---

Variation in median earnings and in the earnings distributions for engineers in the various branches of engineering also is significant. The numbers in Table 2 represent percentiles of earnings, so the lower figure is the median salary of the lowest 10 percent of reported earnings, and the higher is the earnings of those in the top 10 percent of reported earnings. As you can see, the range between high and low earnings is quite significant across the board, which makes it more difficult to describe an average salary for each area of specialty.

Table 2. Median Earnings in Highest and Lowest Percentiles by Engineering Specialty

SPECIALTY	LOWEST 10%	HIGHEST 10%
Aerospace	$52,820	$113,520
Agricultural	$37,680	$90,410
Biomedical	$41,260	$107,530
Chemical	$49,030	$115,180
Civil	$42,610	$94,660
Computer	$50,490	$123,560
Electrical	$47,310	$108,070
Electronics	$49,120	$112,200
Environmental	$40,620	$100,050
Health and safety	$39,930	$92,870
Industrial	$42,450	$93,950
Marine and naval	$43,790	$109,190
Materials	$44,130	$101,120
Mechanical	$43,900	$97,850
Mining and geological	$39,700	$103,790
Nuclear	$61,790	$118,870
Petroleum	$48,260	$140,800

Source: 2005 National Association of Colleges and Employers survey

. . . .
Final Advice

So, what can you do now to polish your skills and explore further the field of engineering? First of all, take every opportunity you can to meet engineers—join professional organizations, conduct informational interviews, and pursue internships and co-op opportunities. Learn about the multinational connections of the branch of engineering you're most interested in and learn one of the languages that could be helpful in writing or speaking with an engineer from one of those countries. If you have the chance to go overseas—even if it's not for an engineering job—take it. The experience alone will give you a leg up on the students around you who don't have any international experience. Learn how to speak in front of a group. It doesn't matter if the only chance you get is talking to peers about not drinking and driving—that counts, and probably more than giving a lecture on acoustics or materials technology. Getting a job in engineering is still tough, and you'll need to know how to learn what a company is looking for, how to translate what you've done into what they can relate to their job opening, and how to explain it to an interviewer in a concise, clear, professional manner. The more comfortable you are in speaking in front of a group, the easier it will be for you to survive an interview without sweating all over your interview suit.

CHAPTER SEVEN

Art Conservators and Restorers

Many people think that once something valuable is housed in a museum it's safe, but unfortunately decay can happen on the museum's walls or shelves just as fast as in a private home. Many conditions contribute to that decaying process: light, variations in humidity and temperature, pollutants, pests, and accidental damage. It's the job of art conservators and restorers to prevent and reverse damage to ancient and valuable objects. These two jobs have very different focuses, but they both require a delicate touch and a meticulous approach to the work. Perfectionists can put their skills to good use in the highly specialized fields of art conservation and restoration.

Art Conservator

Conservators manage, care for, preserve, treat, and document works of art, artifacts, and specimens—work that may require substantial historical, scientific, and archaeological research. They use x-rays, chemical testing, microscopes, special lights, and other laboratory equipment and techniques to examine objects and determine their condition, their need for treatment or restoration, and the appropriate method for preserving them. Conservators document their findings and treat items to minimize their deterioration or to restore them to their original state. Conservators usually specialize in a particular material or group of objects, such as documents and books, paintings, decorative arts, textiles, metals, or architectural material.

An objects conservator for a natural history museum probably sees a wider range of items than the average art museum conservator. For example, he or she might work with a variety of anthropological objects, including animal skins, ceremonial robes, wooden dolls, and feathered headdresses. Many of these garments and items were not meant to last longer than a few years, but some of them have survived several hundred. A conservator's efforts show long-lasting results.

Conservators usually don't do a lot of restoration work; instead, they try to keep an object's integrity intact as much as possible. Restoration often involves an effort to bring something back to the condition it was in when it was new. Conservators, on the other hand, want to slow down further deterioration.

An example of an object with which a conservator might work is a Hopi headdress made of wood with feathers and leather straps. There might also be more elaborate headdresses from the Plains groups, such as the Crow, the Arapaho, and the Lakota (formerly known as Sioux), made with dyed horsehair and eagle feathers that trail from the wearer's head to the ground. A conservator would make sure that the display of these items doesn't further damage them; they might need to be kept behind glass, for example, away from curious hands. The conservator might also remove any chemicals that are causing items to deteriorate. Handling these items requires extreme care because of their delicate condition.

Conservators concern themselves with preventing deterioration through a number of steps:

1. Examination of the object to determine its nature, properties, method of manufacture, and the causes of deterioration
2. Scientific analysis and research on the object to identify methods and materials

3. Documentation of treatment methods and the condition of the object before, during, and after treatment
4. Preventive measures, such as providing a controlled environment, to minimize further damage
5. Treatment to stabilize objects or slow their deterioration
6. Restoration, when necessary, to bring an object closer to its original appearance

Training and Education

Conservators are highly trained professionals who have gone through a number of steps to gain their expertise. When hiring conservators, employers look for a master's degree in conservation or in a closely related field, together with substantial experience. There are only a few graduate programs in museum conservation techniques in the United States. Competition for entry to these programs is keen; to qualify, a student must have a background in chemistry, archaeology or studio art, and art history, as well as work experience. For some programs, knowledge of a foreign language is helpful. Conservation apprenticeships or internships as an undergraduate can enhance admission prospects. Graduate programs last two to four years, the latter years of which include internship training.

A few individuals enter conservation through apprenticeships with museums, nonprofit organizations, and conservators in private practice. Apprenticeships should be supplemented with courses in chemistry, studio art, and history. Apprenticeship training, although accepted, is a more difficult route into the conservation profession.

Careful planning at the undergraduate level will help improve the chances of acceptance into a graduate program, but because acceptance is very competitive, it is not unusual to have to repeat the application process. Before reapplying, however, it is a good idea to enhance your standing by undertaking additional studies or fieldwork. Many programs, on request, review your resume and suggest avenues for further study.

Apprenticeships or internships are a vital part of training and are usually taken during the final year of study. Some programs offer internships that run concurrently with classes. During the course of a training program, student conservators are exposed to working with a variety of materials before going on to specialize in a particular area. They learn skills to prevent the deterioration of paintings, paper and books, fiber, textiles, ceramics, wood, furniture, and other objects. There are even conservators in architectural conservation and library and archives conservation.

According to the American Institute for Conservation of Historic and Artistic Works (http://aic.stanford.edu/), the qualities a conservator must have include:

- appreciation and respect for cultural property of all kinds— their historic and sociological significance, their aesthetic qualities, and the technology of their production
- aptitude for scientific and technical subjects
- patience for meticulous and tedious work
- good manual dexterity and color vision
- intelligence and sensitivity for making sound judgments
- ability to communicate effectively

Admission requirements for the various graduate programs differ, but all of the programs require academic prerequisites, including courses in chemistry, art history, studio art, anthropology, and archaeology. Some programs prefer candidates to already have a strong background in conservation, which can be gained through undergraduate apprenticeships and fieldwork in private, regional, or institutional conservation laboratories. A personal interview is usually a requirement of the application process. A candidate's portfolio must demonstrate manual dexterity as well as familiarity with materials and techniques.

Relatively few schools grant a bachelor's degree in museum studies. More common are undergraduate minors or tracks of study that are part of an undergraduate degree in a related field, such as art history, history, or archaeology. Students interested in further study may obtain a master's degree in museum studies, offered in colleges and universities throughout the country. However, many employers feel that, while museum studies are helpful, a thorough knowledge of the museum's specialty and museum work experience are more important.

For all those working in the field, continuing education is available through meetings, conferences, and workshops sponsored by archival, historical, and museum associations.

Restorer

Restorers preserve and restore a range of damaged or faded objects, including paintings, ceramics, textiles, paper, furniture, weapons and armor, and natural history materials. They apply solvents and cleaning agents to clean the surfaces of the objects, reconstruct or retouch damaged areas, and apply preservatives to protect them. Cleaning and treating the objects can take weeks or months, and the whole process is carefully recorded. Restoration is highly detailed work and usually is reserved for experts in the field because damage to the items could be costly.

Restorers tend to specialize in a particular type of object. The work of a painting restorer, for example, entails preserving and reinforcing the support of a painting (whether on canvas, metal, or wood); removing dirt, varnish, and old discolored restorations; and making the necessary touch-ups and applying a protective coat of varnish. Each one of the operations has many alternative solutions; it is the restorer's job to choose appropriate methods and materials as well as to carry out the work. In addition, restorers are often asked for opinions as to the authenticity and age of a painting. Other aspects of restoration work may include surveying collections to advise on storage and to monitor environmental conditions or setting up exhibitions and displays.

Those who restore furniture do not, as a rule, work in museums. For the most part, these restorers have their own businesses. Furniture restorers working for themselves have more flexibility to define their own career direction, though there are fewer opportunities to specialize than there used to be. Those who start a business often find that gaining private customers can be one of the most challenging aspects in the early stages. It is advisable to start work with a private company at first to gain experience in dealing with customers, as well as to develop useful contacts.

Life on the Job

Now, take a moment to imagine that you're working as a restorer for a natural history museum specializing in Native American artifacts. What exactly is the day-to-day work like? Well, this section will walk you through the work life of a historical artifact restorer.

It's about eight in the morning, and you just received a shipment containing a bentwood box from the Northwest Coast Indian group named Haida. The bentwood box is badly abraded and broken in many places, and someone had previously hammered steel nails all over it. You know that's not compatible with what it looked like in the beginning, but you don't want to begin your conservation work until you document what it looks like now, where the breaks are, and where the new and modern materials have been used on it. Merely describing it as a bentwood box does not say that much about the state or condition of the artifact.

When documenting, you describe the colors painted on the box, the design of it, and the technique that was used to cut out the design. You need to be very specific in describing its flaws, such as, "There's a fracture five millimeters long at the front right corner." During this initial documentation phase, you take photographs of the box to show its condition on arrival. In fact, you end up taking photos of the box before you work on it, during the time you work on it, and then after you're finished. The purpose of all this documentation is to have a historical record of what an object is made of, what you used on it, and why you did what you did in the restoration process.

After documenting the box's original condition, you research the materials it was made from, how it was made, and the nature of colorants—the red, the black, the blue, the green. You carefully take samples of the materials used on the box and send them to a lab for analysis or, if you're trained in this area, you might use your own microscope to try to determine what the origin of the dye or paint was.

After this period of research and documentation, you remove the modern materials that have marred the original look of the box and use adhesives that are reversible, so they don't cause additional damage to the box. You clean off soot and particulates without doing damage to the paint. You also try to disguise the abrasions in the box but without adding modern materials to it because you don't want to obscure the original artist's work. After you're finished restoring the box, you document how it turned out, and it's now ready for display in the museum.

Training and Education

Training for a restorer is similar to that of a conservator. In particular, the basic education required in this highly specialized field is a master's degree or beyond in art history with special training in restoration. Because fine and valuable objects are found all over the world, studying a foreign language may be useful. Finally, you need a solid background in chemistry and physics, as well as training in studio techniques.

If you're interested in working as a restorer of furniture, you need to complete an apprenticeship with an established furniture restorer. Furniture restoring is quite different from restoring ancient artifacts and paintings. Training for furniture restorers follows the more traditional path of apprenticeship and on-the-job training of carpenters and woodworkers.

Work Settings and Hours

Conservators and restorers preserve often valuable items for permanent storage or display. They work for museums, governments, colleges and universities, corporations, and other institutions. They describe, catalogue, analyze, exhibit, and maintain valuable objects and collections for the benefit of researchers and the public. These collections may include works of art, coins and stamps, living and preserved plants and animals, and historic objects, buildings, and sites.

The working conditions of restorers and conservators vary. Some spend most of their time working in labs on their objects, while others perform research, which often means working alone or in offices with only a few people. Those in zoos, botanical gardens, and other outdoor museums and historic sites frequently walk great distances during the course of the day. Those who work for large institutions may travel extensively to evaluate potential additions to the collection and conduct research in their area of expertise. However, travel is rare for those employed by small institutions.

Being a conservator or restorer is a team effort. Very often the conservators working at a facility consult with each other about what they should do with a piece that's damaged, whether to leave it alone or just stabilize it to prevent further loss. Conservators also work with the exhibits department, sharing advice on how to build a mount to support an object, for example. They provide much of the information that is displayed on labels and arrange for proper lighting levels to prevent colors from fading. Conservators work closely with exhibit designers and curators when they're planning a new show or transporting objects. How an object is supported or wrapped for safe transportation to another museum often falls into the conservator's realm. And though interacting with visiting scholars is generally part of a collection manager's job, conservators often instruct students in the correct way to handle an object.

Conservators and restorers may work under contract to treat particular items, rather than as regular employees of a museum or other institution. They may work on their own as private contractors, or they may work as employees of a conservation or restoration laboratory or center that contracts its services to museums. There is much more autonomy in this type of job; often conservators and restorers are able to choose what objects they wish to work on.

Both conservators and restorers work regular hours, usually a forty-hour workweek. Of course, independent contractors set their own schedules, working as few or as many hours as they wish.

Job Outlook

Keen competition is expected for most conservator and restorer jobs because qualified applicants generally outnumber job openings. Graduates with highly specialized training, such as master's degrees and extensive computer skills, should have the best opportunities for jobs. Candidates may have to work part-time, as interns, or even as volunteers or research associates after completing formal education. Substantial work experience in research or restoration and database management skills are necessary for permanent status.

Conservator positions are limited. That's because not every natural history or art museum has a conservator on staff. Very often a museum will send its work to a private conservator because it can't afford to hire a full-time conservator. On the other hand, some museums—typically larger, more prominent museums—employ two or three conservators for fine arts and/or objects. The job outlook for graduates of conservation programs is better than for those who don't go through this formal training. However, competition is stiff for the limited number of openings in these programs, and applicants need a technical background before they're admitted. Conservation program graduates with knowledge of a foreign language and a willingness to relocate will have an advantage over less-qualified candidates.

Conservator and restorer jobs are expected to grow slightly as public interest in science, art, history, and technology increases. Museum and zoo attendance has experienced a drop in recent years because of a weak economy, but the long-term trend has been a rise in attendance, and this trend is expected to continue. There is healthy public and private support for and interest in museums, which will generate demand for these workers. However, museums and other cultural institutions can be subject to cuts in funding during recessions or periods of budget tightening, thus reducing demand. Although the rate of turnover in these jobs is relatively low, the need to replace workers who leave the occupation or stop working will create some additional job openings—maybe even one that's waiting for you to fill it!

....

Salaries

Salaries for art conservators and restorers aren't glamorous. According to government statistics, the median annual earnings of those working in this area are $31,800. The middle 50 percent earn between $23,800 and $43,800. The lowest 10 percent earn less than $18,200, and the highest 10 percent earn more than $58,300.

Salaries for restorers and conservators working for museums and galleries are fairly standard, whereas in the private sector they vary widely depending on competence and years of experience. Starting salaries for those working for the state or federal government tend to be higher than those in the private sector, but at the top of the profession the highest salaries can probably be earned as a private restorer.

A Gentle Touch

Working as a restorer or conservator is ideal for those who consider themselves perfectionists. Not only must you master the information needed during the course of training for your job, but you also must be able to deal with tasks that require a lot of patience. These are professions in which you can never know it all; there is simply too much to learn. Thus, if you do become a successful restorer, you will have more than a job, or even a profession—you will have an absorbing interest that will last you for life.

CHAPTER EIGHT

Researchers

A researcher needs perseverance and an eye for detail and perfection. Researchers sift through an incredible amount of information until they find what they're looking for. They may spend hours looking for the proof that a statement is correct, or they may spend months collecting data in order to advance a scientific inquiry. No matter what the topic being researched, the method is meticulous and precise.

The word *research* is a general term used to describe a wide range of jobs. Indeed, research is a large component of many of the jobs covered in this book. Actuaries, IRS agents, art conservators, surveyors, and writers, to name just a few, are involved in some way with research activity. This chapter focuses on researchers in general and on a small but very interesting subset of the field: genealogy.

Researcher

You may think of researchers as scientists or academics. In fact, research is an element in almost every job, whether dealing with objects, people, or ideas. The goals of a researcher are to present knowledge in a different way, to consolidate facts and assemble them to make a point, to discover new relationships in existing knowledge, or to develop background and authenticity.

Although the nature of research jobs varies widely, there are some traits all researchers have in common. The following is a list of attributes that are likely to result in success in the research field. Do you have any of the following traits?

- curious about how or why something occurs
- persistent in the tasks you undertake
- independent and not easily influenced
- creative and thoughtful
- disciplined and focused when working on a project

Researchers of all persuasions investigate problems, issues, or under-explored topics with the goal of identifying information that advances knowledge about those topics. The choice of the research topic, the way you approach your research (called methodology), and the way you communicate your results all contribute to your success as a researcher.

Research is a systematic means of studying a topic of interest. You follow the scientific method in order to examine something without introducing your own biases or influencing the work in any way. For example, if you develop a questionnaire, you must make absolutely sure that none of the questions are phrased in such a way as to make the person taking the survey respond in a particular way.

There are many ways to gather data during research; polls and questionnaires are just two of them. Some research is gathered by sifting through thousands of documents and examining themes or data. Some researchers watch animals for hours at a time, taking notes on their behavior. Some work primarily in labs, peering into microscopes at cells on slides. There are as many different ways to conduct research as there are topics to study.

How does one decide what to research? Many people get their first taste of research while in college. Usually, college students read research articles when writing papers for classes. It's not until you enter a master's degree program that you begin to conduct research yourself. By the time you enter a master's program, you'll have a set area of interest. You might be inclined toward biology or nursing or marketing, just to name a few. In a master's program, you narrow your area of interest within the broader field of your undergraduate major. In nursing, for example, you might be interested in women's health issues, and in marketing you might favor using new technologies, such as the Internet, to reach people. In order to obtain your master's degree, you choose a research topic and write a thesis supporting your work. This will be your first exposure to the research process and might just launch a career focusing on this area.

Academia

Professors at colleges and universities spend much of their time conducting research and publishing their findings. These researchers have obtained a Ph.D. and have usually completed at least one research study during school while working toward a degree. Initially, professors may start out furthering their research by building on their doctoral dissertations; however, most researchers do not spend their entire careers in one area. Many researchers shift or expand into new areas either early in the tenure process or late, when they have already established themselves in one area.

With research comes publication. Publication in well-respected journals reflects the expertise of the researcher and improves the reputation of the institution. Building a body of research and published material that is visible to others in your area of study is an important part of ensuring that your institution grants you tenure.

Tenure. At this point, you're probably asking yourself: what exactly is this "tenure" you're hearing so much about? Tenure-track positions are the most coveted jobs at universities because they are stable; having tenure means that a professor cannot be fired or let go from his or her position. In order to obtain this level of security, however, a professor must prove the quality of his or her teaching and scholarship by getting published in the most prestigious scholarly journals. This usually takes from five to seven years. After being granted tenure, faculty members may concentrate on conducting new research, setting up academic programs, supervising student research, writing books or articles for publication, or teaching. Before committing to this line of work, you should ask yourself if you are willing to put up with many years of graduate education, years of fieldwork, and then frequent job hunting with no guarantee of a tenured teaching or research position.

Hospitals and Pharmaceutical Companies

Hospitals and pharmaceutical companies are huge employers of researchers. In fact, new research discoveries made by those working in hospitals and for pharmaceutical companies are big business. In the pharmaceutical industry alone, the investment in research reached a record $51.3 billion in 2005! That's because, as a nation, we're incredibly interested in maintaining and improving our health.

The research that occurs in hospital settings focuses on improved treatments or cures for a range of illnesses and diseases. One hospital, for example, might have a dedicated team of researchers studying new treatments for asthma or types of immune-suppressants for organ transplants. Cancer research is one of the most well-funded areas of research within the health care field, along with HIV/AIDS treatment and heart disease. One of the newest areas of research in the hospital setting is biomedical informatics. In this area, researchers are using the latest technology to come up with new diagnostic instruments and software.

Pharmaceutical companies are constantly trying to discover the latest drug or improve upon existing options. In fact, the discovery, evaluation, development, and testing of new drugs is currently one of the most exciting careers in scientific research, ranging from basic biomedical investigation of living cells and molecules to applied research that yields new consumer products to improve health. The medicines and techniques used in medical practice are continually undergoing change, much of which is attributable to the discovery of major new drug groups by pharmaceutical research and development operations. These discoveries are the result of targeted effort, experience, know-how, analysis, teamwork, and serendipity.

Clinical Trials. In clinical trials, teams of physicians carry out studies designed to determine if a drug is a safe and effective treatment for the particular disease being studied. Drugs and treatments must undergo rigorous testing in order to reach the clinical trial stage. Once approved, there are three phases of clinical trials:

- **Phase I:** The medicine is tested in a small group (twenty to one hundred) of healthy volunteers to determine its safety profile, including the safe dose range. Pharmacokinetic studies examine how a drug is absorbed, metabolized, and excreted from the body, as well as how long it takes to work. Phase I studies can take from six months to one year to complete.
- **Phase II:** Placebo-controlled trials involve approximately one hundred to five hundred volunteer patients who have the disease being studied. The goal of this phase is to establish that the medicine effectively treats the disease. Researchers continue to evaluate the drug's safety, look for side effects, and determine optimal dose strength and frequency. Phase II studies can take an additional six months to one year to complete.
- **Phase III:** The medicine is tested in large, randomized, placebo-controlled trials with much larger numbers of patient volunteers (one thousand to five thousand) in hospitals, clinics, and/or physician offices. Researchers closely monitor patients at regular intervals to confirm that the drug is effective and to identify side effects. Phase III studies can take from one to four years to complete,

depending on the disease, the complexity of the study, and the number of volunteers.

At a pharmaceutical company, while the clinical trials are taking place, researchers are also conducting a number of other studies. Researchers in various departments are conducting long-term safety evaluations, making plans for full-scale production, studying package design, and preparing the complex application required to submit to the U.S. Food and Drug Administration (FDA). FDA approval is required in order to manufacture any drug used in the treatment of disease.

Once all three phases of the clinical trials are complete, a company analyzes all of the data. If the findings demonstrate that the experimental medicine is both safe and effective, the company files a New Drug Application (NDA) with the FDA. These applications typically run one hundred thousand pages or longer, which shows just how much testing a medicine must go through in order to gain FDA approval. The applications contain all of the information about the studies, including preclinical testing, clinical trials, dosing information, manufacturing details, and proposed labeling for the new medicine.

Finally, the FDA scientists review all the results from the studies carried out over the years and determine whether they show that the medicine is safe and effective enough to be approved. If the medicine is approved, it becomes available for physicians and patients. It takes an average of nearly seventeen months for the FDA to review each medicine it approves. The proportion of rejected applications has remained constant over the years at about 10 to 15 percent.

Marketing

Marketing is another large area in which a lot of research is conducted. Marketing research is the process of systematically gathering, analyzing, and interpreting data pertaining to a company's market, customers, and competitors, with the goal of improving marketing decisions; in other words, marketing research is conducted in order to better identify and link products to consumers. Marketing researchers might also collect and interpret data on consumer demands and characteristics so that companies can develop new products in addition to selling existing ones profitably. In addition, marketing researchers interpret the market for clients so that companies can minimize waste and develop new sources of profit. Focus groups, telephone polls, surveys, and computer programs that track Internet clicks are the tools of the trade for marketing researchers.

Marketing research is big business in our consumer, capitalist economy. Companies both large and small seek the services of these professionals to help them make better or more strategic business decisions. You might end up working for a large corporation in the marketing department or for an organization that offers marketing services to other companies. In any case, this is an interesting area of research with many opportunities.

Grants

For many researchers, in particular those in the scientific domain, gaining funding for their research is necessary to undertake the research in the first place and is also critical to the success of the project. Funding in the form of research grants is used to support students and staff, to travel to professional meetings and conferences, and to obtain equipment necessary for research. For some researchers, part of the process of collaborative research includes writing grant proposals with their colleagues. You may need to attend a seminar or conference focusing on grant-writing skills in order to become more adept at it.

Job Outlook

The job outlook for researchers varies. Those interested in pharmaceutical research or more specialized scientific research, such as genetics research, will find more opportunities. Business is another strong area for future researchers to enter.

For those interested in working in academia, the number of tenure-track positions has declined in recent years as institutions seek flexibility in dealing with financial matters and changing student interests. Today, colleges and universities rely more heavily on limited-term contracts and part-time, or adjunct, faculty, thus shrinking the total pool of tenured faculty. Limited-term contracts—typically two to five years—may be terminated or extended when they expire and generally do not lead to tenure. In addition, some institutions have limited the percentage of faculty who can be tenured.

For those interested in marketing research, employment growth should be the fastest in private industry, especially in management, scientific, and technical consulting services. Rising demand for market analysis in virtually every industry should stem from the growing global economy, the effects of competition on businesses, and increased reliance on quantitative methods for analyzing and forecasting business, sales, and other economic trends. Some corporations choose to hire marketing research consultants to fill these needs, rather than keeping one on staff. This practice should result in more employment in consulting services.

Training and Education

What degree your employer prefers depends on the setting in which you want to work. Colleges and universities, for example, require applicants to possess doctoral degrees. Preference is usually given to candidates with previous teaching and/or research experience; in particular, academic institutions look for research activities that complement existing programs. Hospitals and pharmaceutical companies also require researchers to possess a Ph.D. as well as experience in the field.

Marketing tends to be less stringent in terms of the degree required to conduct research, especially at the entry level, often requiring only a bachelor's degree in marketing. There is, however, a move by professional organizations to gain certification in order to ensure high standards of research. In particular, the Marketing Research Association (www.mra-net.org) offers the Professional Researcher Certification. This certification was developed for researchers of all levels of work experience and education in order to encourage high standards within the profession, raise competency, establish an objective measure of an individual's knowledge and proficiency, and encourage continued professional development. Certification is achieved by obtaining a certain number of continuing education credits.

Whether working in government, industry, research organizations, or consulting firms, marketing researchers with a bachelor's degree usually qualify for most entry-level positions as research assistants, for administrative or management trainee positions, or for various sales jobs. A master's degree usually is required to qualify for more responsible research and administrative positions. Many businesses, research and consulting firms, and government agencies seek individuals who have strong computer and quantitative skills and can perform complex research. Finally, a doctorate is necessary for top marketing research positions in many organizations.

The key requirement for a life of research is a desire to know and uncover facts. In addition, a researcher (whether scientific, academic, or journalistic) needs persistence, good judgment, empathy, and intuition. A researcher must establish limits and develop shortcuts or the process goes on forever, each step leading to another source, ad infinitum. In general, if you're a student who thrives in an academic environment, you will likely have the curiosity and temperament to excel as a researcher.

Salaries

Salaries for researchers are wide ranging. Salaries for those starting out teaching in colleges and universities aren't glamorous, although achieving tenure and some authority in the field does substantially increase earnings. According to a recent survey by the American Association of University Professors, salaries for full-time faculty averaged $68,505. By rank, the average was $91,548 for professors, $65,113 for associate professors, $54,571 for assistant professors, $39,899 for instructors, and $45,647 for lecturers.

Faculties in four-year colleges or universities earn higher salaries, on average, than do those in community colleges. For example, faculty salaries average $79,342 in private independent institutions, $66,851 in public institutions, and $61,103 in religiously affiliated private colleges and universities. The starting salary for community college teachers ranges from $31,947 to $38,611, depending upon degrees and experience.

In addition to a base salary, many faculty members have significant earnings from consulting, teaching additional courses, doing research, writing for publication, or working in other employment. Many college and university faculty also enjoy some unique benefits, including access to campus facilities, tuition waivers for dependents, housing and travel allowances, and paid sabbatical leaves. Part-time faculty usually have fewer benefits than full-time faculty, however.

According to government statistics, the median annual earnings of market researchers is about $56,100. The middle 50 percent earn between $40,500 and $79,900. The lowest 10 percent earn less than $30,900, and the highest 10 percent earn more than $105,900. Median annual earnings of survey researchers—those who carry out the survey polls and usually have a bachelor's degree in marketing—is about $26,500. The middle 50 percent of those working in these positions earn between $18,000 and $41,400. The lowest 10 percent earn less than $15,300, and the highest 10 percent earn more than $56,700.

Hard data on the salaries of those working in hospital and pharmaceutical research is limited; however, one study showed that pharmaceutical researchers earned a median annual income of $72,330. Hospital researchers might earn slightly less, although the income for these workers is expected to be favorable.

Genealogist

The study of genealogy, tracing family histories, is a popular hobby enjoyed by many in the United States. This is because many people in the United States have family roots in other cultures and countries. Tracking and tracing these familial roots is a great way to understand your history and those of cultures you may or may not be intimately familiar with.

Some genealogy hobbyists take their interest one step further and become self-employed genealogists, helping others research their family trees. These genealogists may run their own small businesses, or they may work for historical societies or libraries. This is such a small segment of the nation's working population that you probably shouldn't consider this a viable career option. It is, however, a great way to begin to practice research without formal education and explore whether or not the methodical work required of research is appealing to you.

Most genealogists are not formally trained, though specializing in genealogy is possible through some university history and library science programs. In addition, a genealogist can become board certified through the Board for Certification of Genealogists (www.bcgcertification.org).

Getting Started

The National Genealogy Society offers the following suggestions for beginners:

1. **Question older family members.** Encourage them to talk about their childhoods and relatives and listen carefully for clues they might inadvertently drop. Learn good interviewing techniques so you ask questions that elicit the most productive answers. Use a tape recorder and try to verify each fact through a separate source.
2. **Visit your local library.** Become familiar with historical and genealogical publications and contact local historical

societies and the state library and archives in your state capital. Be sure to ask libraries for help. Seek out any specialty ethnic or religious libraries and visit cemeteries.

3. **Visit courthouses.** Cultivate friendships with busy court clerks. Ask to see source records such as wills, deeds, marriage books, and birth and death certificates.

4. **Enter into correspondence.** Write to other individuals or societies involved with the same families or regions. Contact foreign embassies in Washington, D.C. Restrict yourself to asking only one question in each letter you send. Include the information you have already uncovered. Include a self-addressed, stamped envelope to encourage replies.

5. **Become computer literate.** Members of the National Genealogical Society (www.ngsgenealogy.org) can participate in a special computer interest section. It encourages the use of computers in research, record management, and data sharing.

6. **Keep painstaking records.** Use printed family group sheets or pedigree charts. Develop a well-organized filing system so you'll easily be able to find your information. Keep separate records for each family you research.

7. **Write to the National Genealogical Society.** Take advantage of the society's forty-six-page book (*Beginners in Genealogy*), charts, and library loan program. You can also enroll in the home study course called American Genealogy: A Basic Course.

Decoding Your Future

The field of research is a rich and exciting one for many people. It involves methodical work and a scientific approach. Although the work can be rigorous, time consuming, and sometimes downright boring, the payoff can be mysteries unraveled and major advancements made in the knowledge of a range of fields. Researchers of all persuasions can truly make a difference—providing a cure for a disease or adding to a company's bottom line. No matter what area you choose, you are sure to discover a rewarding career in research.

CHAPTER NINE

Writers and Editors

The United States supports the largest mass media system of any country in the world, which in turn has generated millions of jobs. If you enjoy reading and writing, you might want to consider a career in some form of publishing. The abundance of choices for perfectionists wanting to work in this wide-open field could almost be daunting if it weren't so exciting.

The field of journalism is perhaps the most obvious path open to those who have writing and editing talent, but no longer does journalism refer only to working in newspapers. It includes syndicates and wire services, television and radio, and consumer and trade publications. And while these outlets provide a home for journalists to report and interpret the news, they also furnish niches for creative writers with a vast array of specialties, as well as editors, agents, entertainers, broadcasters, producers, photographers, computer experts, and other important frontline and support people.

Because there is such a vast range of jobs within the media, and many of those same positions are found in several different outlets, it is more efficient here to examine each outlet as a career path unto itself. While the role of editor, for example, varies to some degree depending upon the setting, many of the same functions are performed and the same skills utilized in newspapers as well as magazines. The definitive question is not whether to become an editor, but in which area you'll find the most satisfaction working. Similarly, a hopeful writer will benefit from knowing the types of assignments and working conditions involved at the different job settings or whether a career as a freelancer is a viable alternative. Never fear, for every interest there is a job and a setting to satisfy it within the publishing domain. The following is just a partial list of job titles within publishing:

Acquisitions Editor
Art Director
Assignment Editor
Assistant Editor
Associate Editor
Author
Book Editor
Bureau Chief
Bureau Reporter
City Editor
Columnist
Contracts Assistant
Copyeditor
Copywriter
Correspondent
Critic
Desk Assistant
Dramatic Agent
Editor
Editorial Assistant
Editorial Writer
Editor in Chief
Electronic Publishing
   Specialist
Executive Editor

Feature Writer
Freelance Editor
Freelance Writer
Internal Publications Editor
Investigative Reporter
Journalist
Literary Agent
Managing Editor
News Editor
Newspaper Editor
News Writer
Photojournalist
Production Editor
Publisher
Reporter
Researcher
Section Editor
Senior Editor
Senior Writer
Staff Writer
Story Editor
Stringer
Technical Editor
Wire Editor
Writer

Newspapers and Magazines

Visit any bookstore or newsstand and you will see hundreds of magazines and newspapers covering a variety of topics—from sports and news to fashion and parenting. There are also many you won't see there—the hundreds of trade journals and magazines written for businesses, industries, and professional workers in as many different careers. These publications all offer information on diverse subjects to an equally diverse readership. They are filled with articles and profiles, interviews and editorials, letters and advice, as well as pages and pages of advertisements. Whether you work for a newspaper or magazine full-time or as an independent freelancer, you will discover that there is no shortage of markets where you can find work or sell your articles.

Newspapers remain one of the most relied-upon mediums for news and information, and they continue to innovate and expand the ways in which they reach consumers. In addition to the traditional printed product, newspapers are delivering content through various channels, including the Internet, cell phones and other mobile devices, and niche publications. Browse through your local newspaper and pay special attention to the features and focus of the news, check out the paper's website, and consider how you might contribute to the production of the paper.

Employment opportunities abound for those who want to work in the newspaper business. Approximately 380,000 people are employed to produce an astonishing fifty-four million newspapers each day. Newspapers are usually organized around the following departments: news, editorial, advertising, production, and circulation. All provide job opportunities for writers and editors.

Positions within magazines are very similar to those found in newspapers, including writers (both freelance and in-house) and editors.

Reporting

A job as a reporter is viewed as a glamorous and exciting Clark Kent/Lois Lane type of existence and probably attracts more applicants than any other spot on a newspaper staff. As a result, competition is stiff; reporters make up less than one-fourth of a newspaper's roster. In real life, reporting is challenging and fast paced with the pressures of meeting deadlines and filling space allotments always looming. For those who like to be one step ahead of the general public in knowing what's going on, however, this is the ideal job.

Whatever the size or location of the newspaper, the job of reporters is to cover local, state, national, and international events and put all this news together to keep the reading public informed. News reporters are assigned to a variety of stories, from covering a major world event to monitoring the actions of public figures to writing about a current political campaign.

Editorial

Major newspapers and news magazines usually employ several types of editors. The executive editor oversees assistant editors, who have responsibility for particular subjects, such as local news, international news, feature stories, or sports. Executive editors generally have the final say about what stories are published and how they are covered. The managing editor usually is responsible for the daily operation of the news department. Executive and managing editors typically hire writers, reporters, and other employees. They also plan budgets and negotiate contracts with freelance writers, sometimes called "stringers" in the news industry. In broadcasting companies, program directors have similar responsibilities.

Assignment editors determine which reporters will cover a given story. Copyeditors mostly review and edit a reporter's copy for accuracy, content, grammar, and style.

In smaller organizations, such as small daily or weekly newspapers or the membership or publications departments of nonprofit or similar organizations, a single editor may do everything or share responsibility with only a few other people.

The goal of the editorial division of the newspaper is to shape the content that's published in each particular section. Newspaper editorial sections vary with size and location but most include at least some, if not all, of the following types of news stories:

Art	Health
Business	International news
Books	Lifestyles/features
Consumer affairs	Local news
Courts	National news
Crime desk	Religion
Education	Science
Entertainment	Social events
Fashion	Sports
Finance	State news
Food	Travel
Foreign affairs	Weather

A job as an editor is considered by many to be a plum position. Although there are exceptions, editors have usually paid their dues as reporters or staff writers. The duties involved depend in part on the section, but there are many responsibilities in common. Editors write articles or supervise the work of staff writers, making assignments, reviewing copy, and making sure attention is paid to space requirements. They also attend editorial meetings and correspond with freelance writers.

There are many perks associated with being an editor: travel editors get to travel, book editors receive free books in the mail to read and review, sports editors go to a lot of the games, food editors get to eat out, society page editors are invited to myriad social events, and so on.

Staff Writers

Staff or feature writers function in much the same way as news reporters but are generally assigned a regular "beat," such as health and medicine, sports, travel, or consumer affairs. Working in these specialized fields, staff writers keep the public informed about important trends or breakthroughs in a variety of areas. Writers in every section of a newspaper can find a way to make an impact.

Contrary to some misconceived notions, feature writers are not assigned only to fluff pieces. While a fashion writer might not do in-depth investigative pieces, a health and medicine writer can. As a writer, it's possible for you to be nominated for the Pulitzer Prize or win other prestigious national awards if your work is of the highest quality.

Work Settings and Hours

Reporters and journalists always have deadlines hanging over their heads. Unlike fiction writers, who can work at their own pace, reporters do not have the luxury of waiting for their creative juices to begin to flow. A news reporter has to file a story, or maybe even two, every day by a certain time. A staff writer or section editor with a weekly column has more leeway, but still, everything must be in on time to go to press.

Reporters gather information by visiting the scene, interviewing people, following leads and news tips, and examining documents. While some reporters might rely on their memory, most take notes or use a tape recorder while collecting facts. Back in the office, they organize their material, decide what the focus or emphasis should be, and then write their stories, generally using a computer. Because of deadlines, while away from the office, many reporters use laptop computers to write the story and then send it by telephone modem directly to the newspaper's computer system.

Some newspapers have modern, state-of-the-art equipment; others do not have the financing they need to update. A reporter could work in a comfortable, private office or in a room filled with the constant noise of computer printers or coworkers talking on the telephone.

Working hours vary. Some writers and editors work Monday through Friday, nine to five, while others cover the evening, night, or weekend shifts. On some occasions, reporters work longer than normal hours to cover an important ongoing story or to follow late-breaking developments.

Although there is some desk work involved, newspaper reporting is definitely not a desk job. Reporters must have excellent interviewing and research skills and the ability to juggle several assignments at once. Computer and typing skills are very important, too.

A reporter also must know how to "write tight." While feature writers can be more creative, news reporters must make sure they cover all the facts within a certain amount of space. The editor might allocate only a column inch or two for a story, leaving room for just the who, what, when, where, why, and how.

Job Outlook

As has been the case historically, the competition will be keen for jobs on large metropolitan and national newspapers, broadcast stations and networks, and magazines. Most job opportunities will be with small-town and suburban newspapers and radio and television stations. Talented writers who can handle highly specialized scientific or technical subjects have an advantage.

According to government statistics, employment of journalists and reporters is expected to grow more slowly than average for all occupations through the year 2014. Many factors will contribute to the limited job growth in this occupation. Consolidation and convergence should continue in the publishing and broadcasting industries. As a result, companies will be better able to allocate their news analysts, reporters, and correspondents to cover news stories. Constantly improving technology also is allowing workers to do their jobs more efficiently, another factor that will limit the number of workers needed to cover a story or certain type of news. However, the continued demand for news will create some job opportunities. For example, some job growth likely will occur in newer media areas, such as online newspapers and magazines. Job openings also will result from the need to replace workers who retire.

Training and Education

By far, most employers prefer individuals with a bachelor's degree in journalism or mass communications, but some hire graduates with other majors. They look for experience at school newspapers and internships with news organizations, so be sure to get some experience in this area in high school and college. Large-city newspapers and stations also may prefer candidates with a degree in a subject-matter specialty such as economics, political science, or business. Some large newspapers may hire only experienced reporters.

There are plenty of options for journalism programs; about twelve hundred schools offer concentrations in communications, journalism, and related programs. About three-fourths of the courses in a typical curriculum are in liberal arts; the remaining courses are in journalism. Examples of journalism courses are Introductory Mass Media, Basic Reporting and Copyediting, History of Journalism, and Press Law and Ethics. Students planning newspaper or magazine careers usually specialize in news-editorial journalism. To create stories for online media, students learn to use computer software to combine story text with audio and video elements and graphics.

Some schools also offer a master's or doctoral degree in journalism. Some graduate programs are intended primarily as preparation for news careers, while others prepare journalism teachers, researchers and theorists, and advertising and public relations workers. A graduate degree may help you advance in your career. You can always go back to school part-time while you're working as a journalist.

You can start preparing for your career in journalism now. High school courses in English, journalism, and social studies provide a good foundation for college programs. Useful college liberal arts courses include English with an emphasis on writing, sociology, political science, economics, history, and psychology. Courses in computer science, business, and speech are useful as well. In addition, fluency in a foreign language is necessary in some jobs.

Reporters typically need more than good word-processing skills. Computer graphics and desktop-publishing skills are increasingly in demand and will definitely set you ahead of the pack. Using and interpreting the results of computer-assisted reporting, which involves using computers to analyze data in search of a story, requires computer skills and familiarity with databases. Knowledge of news photography also is valuable for entry-level positions, which sometimes combine the responsibilities of a reporter with those of a camera operator or photographer.

Employers report that practical experience is the most important part of education and training. Upon graduation many students already have gained much practical experience through part-time or summer jobs or through internships with news organizations. In fact, if you do some research, you'll find that many local newspapers or magazines offer reporting and editing internships. Work on high school and college newspapers, at broadcasting stations, or on community papers also provides practical training. In addition, journalism scholarships, fellowships, and assistantships awarded to college journalism students by universities, newspapers, foundations, and professional organizations are helpful.

There are a range of qualities needed to be a good reporter or journalist. A nose for news, persistence, initiative, poise, resourcefulness, a good memory, and physical stamina are important, as is the emotional stability to deal with pressing deadlines, irregular hours, and, for some, dangerous assignments. All reporters must be at ease in unfamiliar places and with a variety of people.

Most reporters start at small publications or broadcast stations as general assignment reporters or copyeditors. They are usually assigned to cover court proceedings and civic and club meetings, summarize speeches, and write obituaries. With experience, they report more difficult assignments or specialize in a particular field. Large publications and stations hire few recent graduates; as a rule, they require new reporters to have several years of prior experience.

Some editors and reporters can advance by moving to larger newspapers or stations. A few experienced reporters become columnists, correspondents, announcers, or public relations specialists. Others become editors in print journalism or program managers in broadcast journalism. Some eventually become industry managers.

Salaries

Salaries for news editors and reporters vary widely. According to the U.S. Department of Labor, the median annual earnings of reporters and correspondents are about $31,300. The middle 50 percent earn between $22,900 and $47,900. The lowest 10 percent earn less than $18,500, and the highest 10 percent earn more than $68,300. The median annual earnings for salaried editors are $43,900, with the middle 50 percent earning between $33,100 and $58,900. The lowest 10 percent earn less than $25,800, and the highest 10 percent earn more than $80,000. Finally, the median annual earnings for salaried technical writers are $53,500. The middle 50 percent earn between $41,400 and $68,900. The lowest 10 percent earn less than $32,500, and the highest 10 percent earn more than $86,800.

Freelance Writing

Freelance writers sell their work to publishers, publication enterprises, manufacturing firms, public relations departments, or advertising agencies. Some contract with publishers to write a book or an article. Others may be hired to complete specific assignments, such as writing about a new product or technique. A freelance writer works independently, usually writing for several publications. Most freelance writers plan and write articles and columns on their own and actively seek out new markets in which to place them.

More and more magazines are open to working with freelancers these days. With budget cuts and staff layoffs, and because magazines don't have syndicated material to fall back on, it is generally less expensive to pay several different freelance writers by the piece than to employ a full-time staff writer or two.

Some freelancers are generalists; they will write about anything they think they can sell. Others are specialists, choosing to write only in a particular field, such as travel or health and medicine. Successful freelancers have a lot of market savvy; that means they are familiar with all the different publications they could market their work to and know how to approach those publications.

Some freelance writers and editors work in rented office spaces; others work at home and often have to struggle to find the quiet space and time needed to research and write their articles. The search for information sometimes requires that writers travel to diverse workplaces, such as factories, offices, or laboratories, but many find their material through telephone interviews, the library, and the Internet.

Advances in electronic communications have changed the work environment for many writers. Laptop computers and wireless communications technologies allow growing numbers of writers to work from home and even on the road. The ability to e-mail, transmit, and download stories, research, or editorial review materials using the Internet allows writers and editors greater flexibility in where and how they complete assignments.

Some writers keep regular office hours, either to maintain contact with sources and editors or to establish a writing routine, but most writers set their own hours. Freelance writers are paid per assignment; therefore, they work any number of hours necessary to meet a deadline. As a result, writers must be willing to work evenings, nights, or weekends to produce a piece acceptable to an editor or client by the publication deadline. Those who prepare morning or weekend publications and broadcasts also may regularly work nights and weekends.

While many freelance writers enjoy running their own businesses and the advantages of working flexible hours, most routinely face the pressures of juggling multiple projects with competing demands and the continual need to find new work in order to earn a living. Deadline pressures and long, erratic work hours may cause stress, fatigue, or burnout; use of computers for extended periods may cause some individuals to experience back pain, eyestrain, or fatigue.

Training and Education

A college degree generally is required for freelance writers to be appealing to potential publishers. Although some employers look for a broad liberal arts background, most prefer to hire people with degrees in communications, journalism, or English. For those who specialize in a particular area, such as fashion, business, or law, additional background in the chosen field is expected. Knowledge of a second language is helpful for some positions.

Writers must be able to express ideas clearly and logically and should love to write. Creativity, curiosity, a broad range of knowledge, self-motivation, and perseverance also are valuable. Writers must demonstrate good judgment and a strong sense of ethics in deciding what material to publish.

For some jobs, the ability to concentrate amid confusion and to work under pressure is essential. Familiarity with electronic publishing, graphics, and video production equipment increasingly is needed. Use of electronic and wireless communications equipment to send e-mail, transmit work, and review copy often is necessary. Online newspapers and magazines require knowledge of computer software used to combine online text with graphics, audio, video, and animation.

High school and college newspapers, literary magazines, and community newspapers and radio and television stations all provide valuable writing experience as well as "clips," or clippings of articles you wrote for publication that can be useful in selling your services as a writer. Freelance writers don't necessarily need a long, impressive resume to sell that first article—the writing can speak for itself. Still, many publishers ask for your clips to see whether you have what it takes to write for publication.

Many magazines, newspapers, and broadcast stations offer internships for students that also help you gain valuable experience. Interns write short pieces, conduct research and interviews, and learn about the publishing or broadcasting business.

Many freelance writers look for work on a short-term, project-by-project basis. Many small or not-for-profit organizations either do not have enough regular work or cannot afford to employ writers on a full-time basis. However, they routinely contract out work to freelance writers.

Advancement for freelancers often means working on larger, more complex projects for more money. Building a reputation and establishing a track record for meeting deadlines also makes it easier to get future assignments, as does instituting long-term freelance relationships with the same publications.

The growing popularity of blogs could allow some writers to get their work read; a few well-written blogs may garner some recognition for the author and may lead to a few paid pieces in other print or electronic publications. However, most bloggers do not earn much money writing their blogs.

Salaries

Staff writers for newspapers and magazines might have less freedom to choose what they write, but they generally have more job security and always know when their next paycheck will arrive. Freelancers trade job security and regular pay for their independence. Getting a check for an article can be rewarding, but, sadly for new freelancers, the checks might not come often enough and are not always large enough to live on. While staff writers are paid a regular salary (though generally not a very high one), a freelancer gets paid only when an article sells. Fees could range from as low as $5 to $1,000 or more, depending upon the publication. But even with a high-paying magazine, writers often have to wait until the story is published before they are paid. Because publishers work so far ahead, planning issues six months or more in advance, payment could be delayed from three months to a year or more.

To the freelancer's advantage, sometimes the same article can be sold to more than one magazine or newspaper. These resales help to increase income. You can also be paid additional money if you can provide your own photographs to illustrate your articles.

Publishing Houses

The world of publishing is busy and exciting, filled with risks and surprises and, sometimes, disappointments. Without the publishing world, writers would never see their words in print; there would be no magazines, newspapers, or books for the public to enjoy, no textbooks for students and teachers to work with, no written sources for information on any subject. Those in the publishing industry wield a great deal of power. They determine what books and stories will see print and, to some extent, help to shape the tastes of the reading public. It's a competitive business, with financial concerns often determining which books will get published. Editors and agents must be able to recognize good writing and know what topics are popular and what will sell.

For editors and agents, as well as writers, there's nothing more exciting than seeing a book you worked on, whether as a writer, editor, or negotiator, finally see print and land in bookstores. The hope is always that the book will take off and find its way to the bestseller list and into the homes of thousands of readers. Then everyone is happy, from the author and publisher to bookstore owners and the sales team and distributors. But there are only ten to fifteen slots on the various bestseller lists, and with thousands of books published each year, the odds are against producing a blockbuster.

Although some books have steady sales and can stay on the publisher's backlist for years, others don't do as well and can disappear from bookstore shelves after only a month or so. Every book is a gamble; no one can ever predict what will happen. But successful editors and agents thrive on the excitement. In the publishing world, anything is possible.

There can be big differences in the way publishing houses are structured, depending on the size of the company. A small press that puts out only three or four books a year might operate with a staff of only two or three. Each person has to wear many hats: as acquisitions editor, finding new projects to publish; as typesetter and proofreader; as sales manager; as promoter and publicist; as clerk and secretary. The large publishing houses, which for the most part are located in New York City, can have hundreds of employees who are separated into different departments such as editorial, contracts, legal, sales and marketing, and publicity and promotion. Within each department there are a number of different job titles. These are some of the different positions within the editorial department, although often the duties can overlap: editorial assistant, assistant/associate editor, editor, senior editor, acquisitions editor, managing editor, production editor, executive editor, editor in chief, publisher, and president.

Editors for book publishers read manuscripts, talk with writers, and decide which books or stories they will publish and how much to pay for them. Editors also have to read what other houses or publications are printing to know what's out there and what's selling. Once a manuscript is selected for publication, an editor oversees the various steps to produce the finished product, from line editing for mistakes to selecting the cover art and writing copy. Editors also regularly attend editorial meetings and occasionally travel to writers' conferences to speak to aspiring writers and to find new talent.

Education and Training

Most editors have at least a bachelor's degree in communications, English, journalism, or any relevant liberal arts or humanities major. Graduate-level courses in publishing are also available, although few in number. One of the most reputable is the Publishing Institute, held at the University of Denver (www.du .edu/pi). It is also helpful to be familiar with publishing law and contracts and have some editing experience under your belt.

In publishing it's rare for someone to start out as an editor without prior experience. Within a publishing house there is a distinct ladder most editors climb as they gain experience and develop a successful track record. They usually start out as editorial assistants, answering the phone, opening and distributing the mail, and typing correspondence. Some editorial assistants are first readers for their editors; they'll read a manuscript, then write a reader's report. If it's a good report, the editor will take a look at the manuscript. Most editorial assistants learn the process from the editor they work for and then move into editorial positions with more and more responsibility. Advancement to full-scale editing assignments may occur more slowly for newer writers and editors in larger organizations than for employees of smaller companies. Advancement often is more predictable, though, coming with the assignment of more important articles or books.

Salaries

Editors are generally paid a set salary. Although the salary is not dependent week to week on the sales success of the books they choose to publish, an editor with a good track record is likely to be promoted and given raises. Starting pay, however, is not particularly impressive. For those just entering the profession, with no prior experience, it is not unusual to start out at $23,000 a year. After some time and success in the field, however, you might be able to earn substantial money, in the upper $70,000 range and more, if you advance to publisher.

Scientific and Technical Writing

Technical writers put technical information into easily understandable language. They prepare operating and maintenance manuals, catalogs, parts lists, assembly instructions, sales promotion materials, and project proposals. Many technical writers work with engineers on technical subject matters to prepare written interpretations of engineering and design specifications and other information for a general readership. Technical writers also may serve as part of a team conducting usability studies to help improve the design of a product that still is in the prototype stage. They plan and edit technical materials and oversee the preparation of illustrations, photographs, diagrams, and charts.

Science and medical writers prepare a range of formal documents presenting detailed information on the physical or medical sciences. They convey research findings for scientific or medical professions and organize information for advertising or public relations needs. Many writers work with researchers on technical subjects to prepare written interpretations of data and other information for a general readership.

Training and Education

Increasingly, technical writing requires a degree in, or some knowledge about, a specialized field—for example, engineering, business, or one of the sciences. In many cases, people with good writing skills can acquire specialized knowledge on the job. Some transfer from jobs as technicians, scientists, or engineers. Others begin as research assistants or as trainees in a technical information department, develop technical communication skills, and then assume writing duties.

Salaries

Median annual earnings for salaried technical writers were $53,490 in May 2004, with the middle 50 percent earning between $41,440 and $68,980. The lowest 10 percent of technical writers earned less than $32,490, and the highest 10 percent earned more than $86,780. Median annual earnings for technical writers in computer systems design and related services were slightly higher, at $54,710.

According to the Society for Technical Communication, the median annual salary for entry level technical writers was $42,500 in 2004. The median annual salary for midlevel nonsupervisory technical writers was $51,500, and for senior nonsupervisory technical writers, $66,000.

Getting Your Foot in the Door

In the world of newspapers, magazines, and book publishing, some experts advise taking any job you can to get your foot in the door. If you wanted to be an editor, for example, you could start out as a contract assistant, then move into an editorial position and up the ladder to senior editor or higher. If you get yourself in the door and get to know the people in the department for which you prefer to work, your chances are better than an unknown candidate wanting to go immediately into an editorial position.

Another successful method is to take more than the one required college internship. If you can get involved in two or even three internships, you'll make more contacts and have a better chance of lining up full-time employment when you graduate. At the same time you'll be adding to your portfolio and creating impressive specifics to include on your resume.

No matter which area you choose, working as a writer or editor will find you surrounded by perfectionists of all persuasions. Reporters should be dedicated to providing accurate and impartial news; accuracy is important, both to serve the public and because untrue or libelous statements can lead to lawsuits. Both freelancers and those permanently employed have to produce high-quality work because they have editors to report to and deadlines to meet. Editors must know all the rules of grammar; in publishing—an exciting and rewarding field—there is no room for error.

Professional Associations

For more information on the careers covered in this book, contact the appropriate professional associations or related resource listed below.

Number Crunchers

Accountants and Auditors

Accreditation Council for Accountancy and Taxation
www.acatcredentials.org

Activity Based Costing Benchmarking Association
www.abcbenchmarking.com

American Accounting Association
www.aaahq.org

American Association of Attorney-Certified Public Accountants
www.attorney-cpa.com

American Institute of Certified Public Accountants
www.aicpa.org

American Institute of Professional Bookkeepers
www.aipb.com

American Society of Women Accountants
www.aswa.org

American Woman's Society of Certified Public Accounts
www.awscpa.org

Association for Accounting Administration
www.cpaadmin.org

Association of Government Accountants
www.agacgfm.org

Association of Independent Accounting Professionals
www.aiaponline.com

Association of Latino Professionals in Finance and Accounting
www.alpfa.org

Association of Practicing Certified Public Accounts
www.ap-cpa.org

Association to Advance Collegiate Schools of Business
www.aacsb.edu

Federation of Schools of Accountancy
www.thefsa.org

Institute of Internal Auditors
www.theiia.org

Institute of Management Accountants
www.imanet.org

National Association of Black Accountants
www.nabainc.org

National Association of Small Business Accountants
www.smallbizaccountants.com

National Association of State Boards of Accountancy
www.nasba.org

National Society of Accountants
www.nsacct.org

Actuaries

American Academy of Actuaries
www.actuary.org

American Society of Pension Professionals and Actuaries
www.asppa.org

Casualty Actuarial Society
www.casact.org

International Actuarial Association
www.actuaries.org

Society of Actuaries
www.soa.org

Statisticians

American Mathematical Society
http://e-math.ams.org

American Statistical Association
www.amstat.org

International Statistical Institute
http://isi.cbs.nl

National Center for Education Statistics
http://nces.ed.gov

Society for Industrial and Applied Mathematics
www.siam.org

Lawyers

American Bar Association
www.abanet.org

American Civil Liberties Union
www.aclu.org

American Immigration Lawyers Association
www.aila.org

American Intellectual Property Law Association
www.aipla.org

American Judges Association
http://naja.ncsc.dni.us

American Law Institute
www.ali.org

National Association of Criminal Defense Lawyers
www.criminaljustice.org

National Association of Legal Assistants
www.nala.org

National Association of Legal Secretaries
www.nals.org

National Lawyers Association
www.nla.org

National Paralegal Association
www.nationalparalegal.org

Architects

Building Architects

American Architectural Foundation
www.archfoundation.org

American Institute of Architects
www.aia.org

American Institute of Building Design
www.aibd.org

Architecture Research Institute
www.architect.org

Association of Collegiate Schools of Architecture
www.acsa-arch.org

National Council of Architectural Registration Boards
www.ncarb.org

National Organization of Minority Architects
www.noma.net

Restoration Architects

National Trust for Historical Preservation
www.nationaltrust.org

Public History Resource Center
www.publichistory.org

Landscape Architects

American Horticultural Therapy Association
www.ahta.org

American Public Gardens Association (formerly American
Association of Botanical Gardens and Arboreta)
www.aabga.org

American Society of Landscape Architects
www.asla.org

Council of Landscape Architectural Registration Boards
www.clarb.org

Environmental Design Research Association
www.edra.org

Surveyors and Mapmakers

American Congress on Surveying and Mapping
www.acsm.net

ASPRS (American Society for Photogrammetry and Remote
Sensing): The Imaging and Geospatial Information Society
www.asprs.org

National Council of Examiners for Engineering and Surveying
www.ncees.org

National Oceanic and Atmospheric Administration
www.noaa.gov

North American Cartographic Information Society
www.nacis.org

U.S. Army Corps of Engineers
www.usace.army.mil

U.S. Bureau of Land Management
www.blm.gov

U.S. Geological Survey
www.usgs.gov

Engineers

American Chemical Society
www.acs.org

American Institute of Aeronautics and Astronautics
www.aiaa.org

American Institute of Chemical Engineers
www.aiche.org

American Society of Civil Engineers
www.asce.org

American Society of Heating, Refrigerating, and Air-
Conditioning Engineers
www.ashrae.org

American Society of Mechanical Engineers
www.asme.org

Institute of Electrical and Electronics Engineers
www.ieee.org

Institute of Industrial Engineers
www.iienet.org

Junior Engineering Technical Society
www.jets.org

Society of Petroleum Engineers
www.spe.org

Art Conservators and Restorers

American Association of Museums
www.aam-us.org

American Institute for Conservation of Historic and Artistic
Works
http://aic.stanford.edu

Association for Preservation Technology
www.apti.org

Association of African American Museums
www.blackmuseums.org

Association of Art Museum Directors
www.aamd.org

Association of College and University Museums and Galleries
www.acumg.org

International Association of Museum Facility Administrators
www.iamfa.org

Society of American Archivists
www.archivists.org

Researchers

American Educational Research Association
www.aera.net

Association of Independent Research Institutes
www.airi.org

Marketing Research Association
www.mra-net.org

National Academy of Sciences
www.nas.edu

National Association for Biomedical Research
www.nabr.org

Pharmaceutical Research and Manufacturers Association of
    America
www.phrma.org

World Association for Opinion and Marketing Research
    Professionals
www.esomar.org

Genealogists

Board for Certification of Genealogists
www.bcgcertification.org

National Genealogical Society
www.ngsgenealogy.org

....

Writers and Editors

American Society of Journalists and Authors
www.asja.org

American Society of Newspaper Editors
www.asne.org

Association of American Publishers
www.publishers.org

Authors Guild
www.authorsguild.org

Investigative Reporters and Editors
www.ire.org

Magazine Publishers of America
www.magazine.org

National Newspaper Association
www.nna.org

Newspaper Association of America
www.naa.org

Society of National Association Publications
www.snaponline.org

Job-Hunting Resources

For more information about available career opportunities, visit the websites listed below.

America's Job Bank
www.jobsearch.org

Career Builder
www.careerbuilder.com

College Grad
www.collegegrad.com

Hot Jobs
www.hotjobs.com

Job Hunters Bible
www.JobHuntersBible.com

JobWeb.com
www.jobweb.com

Monster
www.monster.com

U.S. Department of Labor, Bureau of Labor Statistics
www.bls.gov

About the Author

A full-time writer of career books, Blythe Camenson works hard to help job seekers make educated choices. She firmly believes that with enough information, readers can find long-term, satisfying careers. To that end, she researches traditional as well as unusual occupations, talking to a variety of professionals about what their jobs are really like. In many of her books she includes firsthand accounts from people who provide expert advice for each occupation.

Camenson was educated in Boston, earning her B.A. in English and psychology from the University of Massachusetts and her M.Ed. in counseling from Northeastern University. In addition to *Careers for Perfectionists*, she has written more than two dozen books for McGraw-Hill.

This edition was revised by a freelance writer specializing in a variety of career topics, from the liberal arts to the sciences.